"[A] disarming memoir [that] seeks the stillness inside the chaos, the union inside duality."

—BBC (from "Ten Best Beach Reads of 2017")

"Captivating. . . . Yogis finds the wisdom everywhere [and] shows that the search for enlightenment, with its storms, lulls, and occasional thrills, is not much different from the search for the perfect wave." —*Publishers Weekly* (starred review)

"*All Our Waves Are Water* seeks profound lessons in the ocean."

—*New York Times Book Review*

"For fellow seekers, Buddha-nature on a surfboard."

—*Kirkus Reviews*

"Yogis seems to have reached as close to enlightenment as anyone ever gets. . . . He mixes science with faith and has a great sense of humor about everything along the way."

—*Surfer* magazine

"Evocative and unpretentious. . . . Wry but engaged. . . . Articulate and genuinely funny." —*San Francisco Chronicle*

"Engaging. . . . As he draws wisdom from Tibetan monks, fellow surfers, and a beloved journalism professor, Yogis infuses *All Our Waves* with a rich mix of spiritual quest and down-to-earth adventurism." —*San Jose Mercury News*

"Insightful, contemplative, and eloquently written, Yogis leaves us to realize that life isn't about that elusive end goal of understanding humanity; it's about the risks we're willing to take in our journey to get there."

—Reza Aslan, author of *No god but God* and *Zealot*

"Jaimal Yogis writes in a fun, engaging style, and the ideas he conveys are timeless. *All Our Waves Are Water* is a great pleasure."

—Sharon Salzberg, *New York Times* bestselling author of *Lovingkindness* and *Real Happiness*

"I'll follow Jaimal Yogis into any ocean, walk whichever road with him, and read everything he writes. It always leads to growth." —Wallace J. Nichols, *New York Times* bestselling author of *Blue Mind*

"Spiritual questing, serious surfing, a little hip-hop, and a significant dose of deep, honest humanity—another perfect Jaimal Yogis book!" —Steven Kotler, author of *West of Jesus* and *The Rise of Superman*

"Jaimal Yogis has done it again: reminded us that our humanity depends on our connection to nature and how much we are willing to risk. It's good to know that there is another brother like him out there in the mountains and on the waves."

—Peter Heller, author of *Kook: What Surfing Taught Me about Love, Life, and Catching the Perfect Wave* and *Celine*

"With stirring honesty . . . [Yogis] skillfully chronicles a journey that took him from India and Jerusalem to the sandy beaches of

Indonesia and Mexico. . . . Surfers are sure to enjoy the author's ode to the perfect ride, but it's the personal reflections that will draw readers." —*Booklist*

"Jaimal Yogis's new memoir will take you on a journey of surfing and spiritual growth. . . . If you've been dreaming of the sand and surf ever since finishing *Barbarian Days*, or if you like books that take on subjects of faith and spirituality, then *All Our Waves Are Water* will have you thinking 'Cowabunga!'" —*Bookish*

"With equal doses of humor, self-deprecation, and well-rendered storytelling, Yogis does a great job making these heady themes accessible and entertaining through personal experiences." —*North Bay Bohemian*

"You don't have to be a surfer to appreciate Yogis's description of looking for the light at the end of a curling tunnel of water as a metaphor for his quest for inner peace." —*Honolulu Star Advertiser*

"*All Our Waves Are Water* is as fine a wave of candid, humble, raw, bare-it-all human wisdom as we have seen in quite some time. . . . Through all of the roads, waters, and mountains Jaimal has traversed on his heart's journey, with this work of shimmering prose he has given us an immeasurably beautiful gift." —*Eastern Surf Magazine*

"Thrust forward by a seeker's hunger to know the force that animates everything and his place inside it, *All Our Waves Are Water* takes us on a stoked and transparent ride through the Himalayas, Bali, Israel, and journalistic Gotham. His eccentric and irresistible characters' voices linger like sages. And Jaimal Yogis does something else astonishing—he brings the holy close."

—Sarah Seidelmann, author of *Swimming with Elephants*

"Jaimal's journey in *All Our Waves Are Water* speaks to all of our sojourns through loss, self-discovery, and an earnest attempt to awaken. Like *Saltwater Buddha*, this book is a privileged view into the life of a true seeker, a contemporary bodhisattva living and loving in the world. It's an ode to water, to the primal and playful art of surfing. Jaimal is a great storyteller and he captivates us with his deeply personal tales of being a flesh and blood and thought and emotion creature working to bring more wisdom to his life and light to the world. It's all there, attachment and craving right alongside renunciation and revelation. This book takes the reader from the Himalayas to Mexico to Israel to New York City to Bali and the inner city of San Francisco. The events of each place reveal a rhythm of humanity and divinity as seamless and natural as the in-breath and the out-breath."

—Arnie Kozak, author of *Mindfulness A to Z* and
108 Metaphors for Mindfulness

"From making momos with a jolly monk in the Himalayas to struggling with relationships and big-wave surfing on the beaches of Mexico, Jaimal Yogis takes us on a humorous, insightful, vulnerable, and ultimately relatable journey to inner peace. This is a spiritual book about a real person dealing with real-world issues, one that can benefit us all in understanding how to surf the waves of everyday life with compassion and contentment." —MeiMei Fox, *New York Times* bestselling author of *Fortytude* and *Bend, Not Break*

"In this deeply wise memoir of an already remarkable life, Jaimal Yogis takes us on a good ride through India, surfing, ancient wisdom, and modern physics, and many practical insights about the waves of life. Authentic, direct, and powerful, this is a beautiful book."

—Rick Hanson, PhD, author of *Buddha's Brain: The Practical Neuroscience of Happiness, Love, and Wisdom*

"Jaimal Yogis has spent a lot of time traveling the world seeking solitary meditation, and *All Our Waves Are Water* is his third, charming chronicle of his adventurous discovery of himself. He continues to excel in the areas where he always has as a writer: gorgeous prose on surfing and nature; accessible, insightful interpretations of spiritual texts and teachers; lighthearted self-deprecation where you least expect it. But what sets his newest book apart, and makes it his most rewarding, is the deep focus on relationships, an unexpected twist for a guy who ran away from home in his teens."

—Mark Lukach, author of *My Lovely Wife in the Psych Ward*

"Jaimal takes us on a raw, real, and sublime ride through essays of his life journey around the world to understand the ocean in a drop through the story of his teachers in human and wave form and to find what unites us."

—Shiva Rea, surfing yogini and author of *Tending the Heart Fire: Living in Rhythm with the Pulse of Life*

ALSO BY JAIMAL YOGIS

SALTWATER BUDDHA
THE FEAR PROJECT

ALL OUR WAVES ARE WATER

STUMBLING TOWARD ENLIGHTENMENT AND THE PERFECT RIDE

JAIMAL YOGIS

HARPER WAVE

An Imprint of HarperCollinsPublishers

FIRST HARPER WAVE PAPERBACK EDITION PUBLISHED 2018.

Designed by William Ruoto

Library of Congress Cataloging-in-Publication Data has been applied for.

ISBN 978-0-06-240518-0 (pbk.)

21 22   LSC   10 9 8 7 6 5 4 3

For Pa
1946–2016

Fear is the cheapest room in the house.
I'd like to see you living in better conditions.
—HAFIZ

A BRIEF NOTE ON GOD

od is in this book. And this, I suppose, shouldn't come as a surprise. God is, they say, in all things. But the G-word is loaded (in more ways than including everything throughout time and space). Allow me to briefly explain.

My last book, *The Fear Project*, was about the neuroscience of fear and courage, as well as my own attempt to get over the fear of surfing thirty-foot waves at a break called Mavericks. Having been beaten up by those waves, I cannot highly recommend that project. But before that, I wrote *Saltwater Buddha*, a coming-of-age memoir about running away from home to surf then nearly becoming a Zen monk. Scientists and Zen Buddhists rarely say "God." If they pray to a supreme being, intelligence, or force, they do so silently or while coughing. But I don't think Zen and science are antithetical to God. I have long prayed to the big man or woman. And this book is, at least in its second half, an attempt to explain why.

Before going further, I will note that I was raised by Buddhist-yogi parents who'd largely abandoned their native Judaism (Mom) and Catholicism (Dad) but always hung on to a respect for both. Mom and Pa named me after their '70s Yoga guru, Baba Jaimal Singh—Mom thankfully convincing Pa to drop the "Baba." Our Lithuanian last name,

Yogis, seems to be coincidence. But since Lithuanian is the closest European language to Sanskrit—and Mom practically needs an ambulance if she eats a chili flake—we've often joked that our ancestors were yogis who fled India to escape spicy food.

In any case, if the name Jaimal is making you picture me as a black man—or the Buddhist-yogi history is conjuring images of my family as shiny, happy, furry people raising goats in Mendocino—stop. Goats would have been lovely. And I can grow a decent afro thanks to the Jewish roots. But, much to the chagrin of my hip-hop-obsessed twelve-year-old self, I'm white. Also, my dad was an air force colonel. My mom ran a day care out of our suburban house before becoming a college counselor. We drove a Lincoln station wagon that broke down as often as it ran.

But goats in Mendocino or not, yoga and meditation have always been part of the Yogis family. And even though Buddhists like to frame themselves as sort of intellectually above a creator—since I'm married to a Catholic and have lived with both Yogic and Buddhist masters of different sects—this strikes me largely as good marketing on the part of Buddhists to distinguish themselves from rival yogis. It has also been good marketing for yogis to include the Buddha in their pantheon of saints. Ancient India was a competitive place.

Beyond the salesmanship of religion, however, there's no getting around the fact that the Buddha was a yogi. And as a religion major who has spent far too much time debating such things, I know that if you really press Buddhists on it, most will admit that the difference between their no-tion of "true nature" or "Buddha nature" (infinite, present in all things) and the "God" that Saint Francis, Gandhi, Hafiz, Rumi, or Thomas Merton spoke of (infinite, pres-ent in all things) is likely more of a tomayto-tomahto issue than a theological debate.

That's not to say there aren't huge differences between faiths, philosophies, paths. Or that there aren't some people who think of God as a big Santa Claus in the sky putting people on the naughty list. Everyone is entitled to their view. But we are not concerned with those views in these pages. We are concerned with the whole enchilada, the Big G, the nondual, the substratum of all things, the primal beingness that gives rise to (and *is*) science and poetry, faith and skepticism, supernovas and subatomic particles, Red Sox and Yankees.

In Yoga philosophy, as with all the great faiths, God could never be captured in words. But if you tried, you might say God is an intelligence akin to the Force in *Star Wars* or what Voltaire seems to have been getting at when he wrote that "God is a circle whose center is everywhere and circumference nowhere."

I know there are as many Yogic philosophies as there are scientific theories. Samkhya, Vedanta, Tantra. There is probably now a Yoga philosophy they sell exclusively on-line for just $99.99 with a limited edition organic recycled yoga mat. Humans love to brand and argue. But the truth of our original nature must be singular. And yogis would note that meditation, religion, service, science, philosophy, and those funny pretzel poses are all paths to God. But none of these paths or methods encapsulates God. And none is better than the others. The paths are simply fingers pointing at the moon, rafts across the ocean of suffering, different strokes for different folks. Or to use my favorite metaphor, the paths—like all things subject to birth and death—are waves.

God is the sea.

INTRODUCTION

> *Patch the wind in the pines*
> *To your hempen robes;*
> *Use the moon as a pillow,*
> *The ocean waves as your sheet.*
>
> **—SHIDO MUNAN**

ehind the mist, up north, Mount Tamalpais is opaque. To the south, save a single-file swirl of pelicans, nothing but water and white. Westward, I climb the dunes through drizzle, squinting out on a blackish Pacific.

Having slept on the floor again last night—my hand wedged between crib bars to link fingers with Eben—I stand on these ice-planted dunes in the same clothes I wore yesterday. Brown corduroys caked with splotches of neon-green puff paint. Wrinkled plaid shirt with crusty peanut butter on the cuff. Moccasins. I yawn, scratch my curls, surveying the conditions.

Barely dawn but April has arrived with its usual bluster. Ornery onshore gusts picking up force. Winter's brawn dwindling to flits and splats.

Not that the sea isn't always sublime in its way. I can't often look at it without hearing echoes of Issa:

> *Mother I never knew*
> *Every time I see the ocean*
> *Every time*

But when you peer out from the same dunes each morning, you begin to notice Mom has mood swings. Today she looks to have woken up on the wrong side of the bed.

I sip my coffee, groggy. I don't want to paddle out. After a weekend of two predawn trips to the emergency room—first for Amy who thought she was miscarrying our third boy, then for Eben (boy two) with a 103-degree fever—I don't want to do much. But exercise is parent medicine. I know this. So I meander back across the Great Highway to our little blue house with white trim—the house that's too small for five, the house we narrowly afford—through the garage that looks like a Tetris experiment, tug on the dank five-millimeter wetsuit, grab the nine-foot hull, and trudge back to Ocean Beach, San Francisco.

Wading through the shallows, I'm not thinking about surf. I'm thinking about Amy (thankfully, she wasn't miscarrying but is still miserably nauseous). I'm thinking about work (students need their short stories back). I'm thinking about Mom's hip surgery, Pa's lung cancer traveling to the brain.

Worries congeal. Clumps of dead jellies onshore. But as I lie down to paddle, the first burst of icy brine hits skin. The second. The third. A harbor seal pokes its cheeky head up. Sea foam crackles the ears. Suddenly, out of necessity, I can't think about any of it. Now I'm paddling toward the rip that will carry me through. Now I'm slipping under the "timeless waves," as Seamus Heaney called them. Now the horizon goes and goes.

Beyond the breakers, the chop is absurd. The waves are awful, at least in terms of this wave-sliding game Hawaiians dubbed a sport of kings. But the longboard—foam canoe that it is—will pick up any hint of push. So I turn, paddle, and drop down the muddled face.

A quick burst. Ten yards if I'm lucky. I'm nearly pitched. But success or failure is not the point here; and as I paddle back, this odd ritual—grown man chasing fleeting bursts of salt water purely for fun—starts, again, to work. Senses move from fuzzy to high-definition. Brain and lungs and heart begin to tingle. And with each silly surge, I am lighter: a boy chasing fireflies instead of a father chasing to-dos.

"Did sea define the land or land the sea?" asks Heaney in the same poem I quoted previously. Water, scientists say, gave life as we know it. But then, didn't water need earth to catch it in its gravitational tractor beam?

Geologists and astronomers used to think so. They guessed that water first greeted dry earth hundreds of millions of years after the planet's formation. But recent studies of meteorites said to be old as the sun show large amounts of water actually *inside* them, suggesting, as geologist Horst Marschall told *National Geographic*, that "Earth's water most likely accreted at the same time as the rock. The planet formed as a wet planet with water on the surface."

"The Supreme Good is like Water," wrote Lao Tzu more than twenty-five hundred years ago, "which nourishes all things without trying to." Buddhists offer bowls of water as symbols of the enlightened mind. Conversion to Judaism requires *tevilah*—full immersion into "a body of living waters." *Wudu* is the ritual bathing Muslims perform before praying. And for Christians in the Middle Ages, holy water was so powerful that churches locked up their fonts so the blessed liquid wasn't stolen by sorcerers.

But whether you follow a spiritual path, a scientific one, neither, or both, water has been here. And we've been well pickled. Wallace J. Nichols, a marine biologist, writes that "human fetuses still have 'gill-slit' structures in their early stages of development." And "in its mineral composition, the water in our cells is comparable to that found in the sea."

To boot, the amniotic fluid we bathe in and breathe for nine months is 99 percent genetically identical to seawater. We have too much subcutaneous fat to solely be landlubbers. We also have the ability, like cetaceans, to slow our heart rate while diving to profound depths (some 831 feet without oxygen by the latest free diving record).

Nichols's book, *Blue Mind*, is a riff on why our brains, themselves 80 percent water, show increased happiness and feelings of unity while submerged. So maybe it's just my aqua brain returning home for supper. Or maybe it's the way the fog is wrapping everything in its fat wet quilt. But as the sea buoys my liquid cells, this character I perceive as fixed—writer, surfer, husband, dad—begins to bend. Maybe dissolve.

I don't vanish like some video game ninja. I feel my borders. Bones and blood and teeth all wrapped by this weathered cloak—"skin bag," as the Zen poets called our rubbery exterior. But it's as if I'm ferried to a memory before amoebas struggled, birth by birth and death by death, toward life's most recent neat trick: self-consciousness.

Words have a hard time with the experience. But back in our living room, toddlers attached to shivering legs while I brew another pot, I flick at whatever just happened with memorized stanzas.

> *And all the while my heart shall be*
> *With the bulge and nuzzle of the sea.*

Psychologists say blending into our surroundings is a feature of having thin boundaries versus thick ones. In decades of studies, thick-boundaried people see themselves as part of firm groups ("we do this; they do that"). They see the world as separated into good and evil. They don't recall dreams well or feel unified with the diversity of the world.

Thin-boundaried people remember many, often wild, dreams. The borders between self and other fall away from time to time. It's easier for them to feel empathy, but the thin-boundaried sometimes struggle to stay focused.

I'm on the thin side. As a ten-year-old, I dreamt of living in an African tribe and bawled upon waking, complaining to Mom that the suburbs were less real than tribal life. Her response was that I still had to vacuum the house before I went skateboarding in fake suburbia. I'm not sure if boundaries explain why, at times, I've felt as though everyone and everything out there is actually in here and vice versa. But I know that I'm far from alone.

"One moon shines in the water everywhere," wrote Ch'an (Chinese Zen) master Yung Chia (said to have died peacefully while meditating in 713). "All the reflected moons are just that one."

Rumi, the great Sufi poet, put it like this: "We are not a drop in the ocean. We are the ocean in a drop."

This book is, in essence, an attempt to understand the ocean in a drop, to find that one moon shining in the water everywhere. An attempt to find God, enlightenment—or whatever your preferred word is for the principle that unites us. It's a continuation of my first stumbling-toward-enlightenment book, *Saltwater Buddha*, in which I started off as a starry-eyed sixteen-year-old on probation for theft and drunk driving, and then ran away to Hawaii with little more than a copy of *Siddhartha*, a boom box, and enough cash for a used surfboard.

This one picks up shortly before *Saltwater* ended. And

I meant it to carry on through the years until now. Books have a life of their own, however, and the characters from life in my twenties soon enveloped it.

Readers of *Saltwater Buddha* will recognize some of the terrain—New York, especially—but these pages, even when they overlap in time, are different, especially because I have widened the frame. All memoirs build a container that's something of a lie. (You can never say it all.) But this book gets a little closer to the truth in that surfing and Zen are just big characters among many. The first third of this book takes place as far from ocean as you can get, the Himalayas. There is also a good long section set in a Franciscan friary in Washington Heights; another, in the dusty streets of Jerusalem.

If you came for surfing, you can easily skip to Mexico and Indonesia. But if you can venture onto land for a few chapters, the sea can be found on those snowcapped peaks too. Whatever path you take, though, the great religion scholar Mircea Eliade wrote, "In water, everything is 'dissolved.'" And I'm hoping that this salty-sweet brine we're soaking in blends these tales into something beyond mere letters representing words representing ideas representing experience. There is a place beyond *all that* which also gave birth to *all that*, a place that gathers us in for a really good party. I hope to meet you there.

1

You can fall a long way in sunlight.
You can fall a long way in the rain.
The ones who didn't take the old white horse
Took the morning train.

—ROBERT HASS

t was 3:00 a.m. and spring when I arrived in McLeod Ganj, a sixteen-hour bus ride from Delhi.

Delhi had been 115 degrees. Before arriving there, I'd spent a week in Gujarat, the birthplace of Gandhi, reporting on Hindu-Muslim violence and getting diarrhea. So looking at this quaint Himalayan village glowing with the golden lights of Tibetan monasteries—patches of late-March snow reflecting moonlight—I felt like I'd found refuge. Or, at the very least, a cool rest stop.

At about six thousand feet, the valley was lush but protected by white peaks so immense they looked like staircases to the stars. One mountain, the 18,500-foot Hanuman Ka Tibba, towered on the horizon as grand as the mischievous monkey god it was named after. And though I'd been exhausted from the breakneck ride, I was suddenly so excited to be here I decided to wander until the sun came up.

After Tibet's failed uprising against China in 1959, India allowed the fleeing fourteenth Dalai Lama to make McLeod headquarters for the Tibetan government in exile. Thousands of Tibetan refugees followed, spackling the hillsides with monasteries, hermitages, and centers for Buddhist study.

Of course, the Dalai Lama's presence has also made the village an international pilgrimage site, bringing the inevitable kitsch. Next to a gallery of traditional Tibetan paintings, I found a tourist shop that sold T-shirts with slogans like "My karma ran over my dogma" and "Reincarnation is making a comeback."

When I arrived in India a few months ago, this shop might have pissed me off. Like every other twenty-three-year-old who flees east, I wanted authentic India—not the one packaged for Westerners having a midlife crisis. But by this point, I'd also come to grips with the fact that globalized India *was* authentic India.

In Bangalore, for example, the city I'd first traveled to for a journalism course, I was having a hard time finding a yoga class that wasn't taught by an American in Lululemon tights. Frustrated, I asked a local couple in matching Lacoste shirts where all the Indian yoga teachers were. "Oh, foreign teachers are all the rage," the woman said in a thick South Indian accent. "With those *swamiji* types it's tough to get a good workout."

Thinking this was an urban issue, I then traveled to a remote ashram to see a guru with a reputation for orthodoxy. But after a four-hour bus ride, I was informed that the guru had passed away. His replacement, though Indian, was a retired NASA scientist who led our yoga retreat in PowerPoint.

I'd been in India for about three months now and still occasionally caught myself in eddies of nostalgia for the old country. But I got through those moments by reminding myself that the point of finding that India would be to learn what the ancient yogis taught: life is flux; embrace impermanence. So, instead of resenting the ugly T-shirt store, I took a breath and considered coming back to buy one for my military-officer dad. It said, "You can't handle the meaning of life!"

At the center of town, attached to a monastery adorned with paintings of Buddhas birthing from lotus flowers, I soon came upon a row of red and gold cylindrical prayer wheels. Each wheel was inscribed with the Sanskrit mantra *Om Mani Padme Hum*. I had nowhere to be. So I found myself pacing, spinning the wheels, and reciting the sacred phrase.

In Sanskrit, *mantra* means "mind protection" because it keeps the untamed mind from slipping into heedlessness. But *Om Mani Padme Hum* is special. It's an homage to Avalokiteshvara, the bodhisattva of compassion. Known as Guan Yin in China, Chenrezig in Tibet, Kannon in Japan, and Lokesvara in Cambodia, the bodhisattva is depicted as both male and female, God and Buddha, depending on which tradition you follow. But all these traditions agree that Avalokiteshvara is the embodiment of limitless compassion that runs through—even composes—reality like omniscient electricity. Tibetans often repeat the mantra 108 million times at a stretch, a task that takes several months and is believed to purify the chanter's karma while accessing an infinite well of love in the heart.

"That compassion for all beings is what makes us achieve peerless happiness up to enlightenment," wrote Lama Yeshe, "to be able to do perfect works for others."

All beings have the potential to tap this compassion, the texts say, to awaken here and now. Our Buddha nature is said to be our most basic state, obscured only by our own hardened hearts and narrow thinking. But Tibetans are practical people. Not everyone has months to sit around chanting, which is why these prayer wheels come in handy.

At the core of each wheel stands a small wooden cylinder, or "life tree," inscribed with thousands, even millions, of mantras. A single turning of the wheel is thought to shine millions of these sacred syllables out into the darkness—a sort of flashlight of grace for suffering beings scattered, many Buddhists say, through universes as numberless as sands of the Ganges.

As a college senior who had recently swapped a marine biology major for philosophy and religion (but was currently focused on a minor in journalism in hopes of one day working), I didn't know if I believed that. But as I recited, paced, and spun the prayer wheels, I thought I felt some of the love. Perhaps it was the sleep deprivation, but these mountains seemed on their own space-time curve. Hours seemed to pass like minutes. And before long, the sky was becoming deep purple, then silver blue. Maroon-robed monks and nuns began bustling about the streets, buying cheese and vegetables, and I felt glad there were so few Indians about. Not that I had anything against Indians. I just loved one Indian far too much.

Sati—my girlfriend of three years with whom I'd first planned this trip—had left me for someone else just a month before the departure date. Currently Sati was a three-day train ride south in Bangalore. She was teaching poor village women about hygiene. But any flash of a young woman in a sari could make me think she'd returned, magically, for me. The perfect ending to our Bollywood film.

Sati's parents had disliked me—at least as the guy their daughter was sleeping with. I suspected this was because I wasn't Indian or Hindu. So it made things worse that the man Sati was trading me in for was both. It irked me even more that his name, Jyanth, sounded a lot like "giant."

But it was also poetic justice. In the beginning of our three-year relationship, I'd broken Sati's heart when I decided to go to the University of Hawaii to focus on the important things (surfing, surfing, more surfing) instead of staying in Berkeley, going to antiwar protests, and discussing Edward Said far more than is healthy.

Sati was fervent about fighting for the poor and oppressed, a quality that had helped me fall for her in the first place. But her focus on the external often clashed with my passion for the meditative—not to mention my obsession with spending all my nonmeditating free time chasing surf. Sometimes it felt as though we would forever be circling opposite ends of a yin-yang symbol.

Which was ironic. The only spiritual center my family had attended with any regularity was an ashram in the Sierra Nevada foothills founded by Yogananda, the man often credited with bringing yoga to the United States. With shiny-eyed vegans freshly back from pilgrimages along the Ganges, I remember singing "I am a bubble, make me the sea" over harmonium and tabla. My parents' participation at the ashram waxed and waned through their divorce. But the feeling of the place—particularly that chant—ingrained itself in me. I grew up believing that enlightenment was individual consciousness merging with universal. A ripple experiencing itself as sea.

Sati's parents, being Hindu, were raised with this perspective too. But they'd left India largely to make money. Her father's idea of bliss seemed to be a whiskey and a seven-hour cricket match. Sati's folks seemed to want less talk of inner peace and more of Sati's future 401(k).

My parents, both from East Coast families, had turned to Indian mysticism for freedom from the rat race. Then they scrambled to find practical jobs when macrobiotic restaurants and ashram hopping couldn't support my sister and me. Not surprisingly, Sati's family was now quite a bit wealthier than mine (we still considered Sizzler pretty fancy). But Sati often said she felt a spiritual void and even wondered aloud if she'd fallen for me to fill it.

There were many things to love about Sati. Too many. But one of them was that I needed her practicality to make it to graduation—a task I was finally nearing the end of here in India.

The smells of cardamom and rickshaw diesel began to fill the streets. I went to the first breakfast café open, and after a bowl of *tsampa*, Tibetan barley meal, fatigue set in. Down the street, a gray motel with a distinct Soviet-bloc aesthetic offered rooms for two US dollars per night. I was so tired I didn't care about decor. I paid the clerk, a Kashmiri boy who looked not much older than eleven, wandered into my eight-by-eight cube, and fell into a deep sleep.

The nap became a nonsensical dream. All emotion and no plot. Flashes of Sati's face mixed with twisted lights, shouts, sadness, anger. I woke exhausted, unable to re-member details except for a single comment in my dad's voice: "Sati is stuck at a red light." Whatever peace I'd found under last night's stars was gone. My chest was tight. I felt like screaming, crying, and fighting at once.

I knew the dream was right. Sati was stuck. She couldn't make a decision between Jyanth and me. She'd told me as much at the start of this trip when I visited her gated apartment complex in Bangalore. But there seemed to be a deeper stuckness too. Sati's parents were jovial and kind. They loved her as dearly as any good parents. But having themselves been arranged into marriage, they held more traditional views about love and career. Sati had an open dialogue with them in her quest to be a modern, independent Indian American twenty-four-year-old. This was a woman who'd proudly studied feminist theory at Berkeley. Still, Sati often told me that her parents' ideas—who she should marry, what job she should pursue—clouded her ability to discern what she really wanted for herself.

I was, of course, trapped in many ways by my own family history. But it's easier to see flaws in others. I'd seen Sati's parents hovering over her decision making from our first date. Frustrated as I was with her not choosing me, I was more frustrated with the fact that I couldn't trust my gut and let go.

There was a steep switchback above town that led to a trekking trail, and I shot up it without caring where it led. After about twenty minutes, I was above the tree line, and the sparsity up here—gray rock, snow, sky—made me feel a tinge more like a mountain goat than a weighty human. I walked for another mile or so, panting from the elevation. But the trail soon ended and I found myself sweating and buckled over at the edge of a precipice. I'd heard there were Tibetan hermits and sadhus meditating in the nearby caves. But none were visible. So I decided to do what I'd been wanting to do for months. I screamed from the edge. I growled, wailed, grunted. I even jumped up and down, cursing at my heart for being unable to unhinge itself from the shackles of romantic love.

"Let fucking go!" I shouted. "Let fucking go, you fucking bastard!"

It felt good to be angry. Angry was honest. And alone up here, it felt as though these mountains and sky could absorb anger and transform it all into thunderclouds that would moisten the crops. It seemed these peaks could absorb the whole universe and that was why people came here year after year—to clear out. See what remained.

There was a flat granite rock near the edge of the cliff. I climbed on top of it, crossing my legs and straightening up. My heart was still shut. I still felt like sending Sati a video of me weeping—let her see what she'd *done*. But I also felt a glimmer of hope. There might still be a lifeline here.

Please?
God?
Buddha?
Anyone?

2

When we were just old enough to sort of understand what meditation was—pretending to be a Buddha statue, right?—probably six or so, my sister, Ciel, and I, dressed in our panda bear pajamas, used to meditate with my parents occasionally. Usually this meant giggling so much we'd get kicked out of our little spare room, which functioned as a study and yoga room. That early introduction never turned into habit. Ciel's and my youth was focused on water polo, parties, snowboarding, and *The Goonies*.

When the average popularity contest of high school failed to bring lasting happiness, I tried a variety of plans to escape suffering: drugs, sex, running away to Hawaii, spending my senior year in France to live like a Syrah-swilling existentialist. When none of these worked terribly well, after graduation, I went to live in an orthodox Buddhist monastery to give this whole end-suffering-in-the-mind stuff a go.

I thought I'd gotten a slight head start with meditation. Even if I'd never put any work into it, I must've absorbed some skills by being named after a yogi. Or, you know, through osmosis.

Instead, I could barely sit still for ten minutes without feeling as if someone had my knee in a vise grip. I still remember finishing my first intensive meditation retreat when I was about nineteen. At the close, a group of my friends, all college age, joined a senior monk from Vietnam to decompress from the week of silence. Before we could ask any questions, the monk, Heng Da Shr, looked at each of us as if giving a psychic reading and told us something we needed to work on.

"You're getting lost in planning about school," he told Max, a sophomore who had a couple years' experience with Zen. "Bring your focus back to the belly. Hold the *w'a tou*"—meaning koan.

"Focus on compassion," he told Stella. "You're worrying a lot about your family."

Everyone seemed to have something cool to work on in their practice. Then Heng Da got to me. "You're just in a lot of pain," he said. "Stretch out more."

He was right. Peaceful was not the word for my meditations. It took months to be able to sit remotely comfortably. And once I'd spent hours a day stretching and had the sitting part kind of covered, keeping the body still was a million times easier than dealing with my internal world.

You think when you start meditating you're going to be dealing with something epic—the dissolution of ego, an out-of-body experience perhaps. I found myself having to rewatch every episode of *Mork and Mindy* and *The Cosby Show* and every game of the entire Joe Montana–Steve Young 49ers era. Even during subsequent winter zen sessions when the TV memories began fading to static, my mind never stilled. In the most blissful, quiet moments—

the breath so soft it almost wasn't there—faint ripples of thought and desire still appeared and passed away. The state is called *savichara samapattih* in the Yoga Sutras, meaning "with subtle thought."

Had I stayed on retreat longer, the next level would have been *nirvichara samapattih*, "without subtle thought," and then further absorptions into completely objectless concentrations, *samadhis*, states that are beginning to be measured neurologically, and in which meditators say they become so clear, so absorbed in now, they are not aware of any separation from infinity.

Attaching to these pleasant states can become another pitfall on the path, the texts warn. I was just trying to make it through retreat with fully functioning knees. Still, I cherished the glimpses. Needed them. Those moments of relative calm brought a new contentment. A sort that wasn't dependent on the weather, popularity, or report cards. It just *was*.

But that was when I lived in a monastery, protected from the heroin-laced razors of young love. And there is a maintenance aspect to mindfulness. Now that I was here in the utopia of meditation—sitting in lotus on a Himalayan slab—that unaffected peace seemed like something I'd invented. After I had spent most of the last three months trying to rustle up journalism stories in religious war zones (not the best way, it turns out, to recover from a breakup), meditation seemed anachronistic, even futile. Thoughts of despair cascading down like relentless dominoes.

But I needed to do something. I was broken. And I had

a thread of faith left from those old days. So I forced myself to keep still. I pretended my mind was the sky. And after being carried away dozens of times into the same old cyclones and thunderheads—what I should have done to keep Sati, what I might do to get her back, what a miserable ass I was for leaving her at the start—I kept reeling my focus back to what was here. Stone cliffs, thin air, breath.

And after a time, the dominoes sort of, kind of, began to find space, until some of them maybe didn't always touch. There were—yes, I could sense them ever so faintly—slight breaks in the sequence. And each break felt like a sweet drop of rain in a parched desert.

Slowly. Slowly. Muscles and chest and jaw unwound. And when I opened my eyes, this Himalayan valley looked a little different. It had always been beautiful. But now it also looked as it did the night before under the moon. A place to start over.

Icicles began forming on the granite, and I wandered back down the switchbacks into the village. More tourists were arriving for the Dalai Lama's upcoming teaching, and as I had been annoyed by the T-shirt store, I would have normally been annoyed by all these white people with designer yoga mats. They were another reminder that I was one of them rather than an epic explorer in Peter Matthiessen's *Snow Leopard*.

But tonight, the fellow lost souls were kind of comforting too. Several passersby looked far worse off than me (tough times often drive folks to the Himalayas). But also the sheer number of travelers—so many looking desperate, in some sense, for real love, real anything—sent me into fantasies of falling in love here all over again. The ultimate distraction.

I was not, however, about to fall in love again. I was about to meet a heartbroken monk who wanted to sing.

3

We asked the captain what course
of action he proposed to take toward
a beast so large, terrible, and
unpredictable. He hesitated to
answer, and then said judiciously:
"I think I shall praise it."

—ROBERT HASS

For the first thirty-eight hundred thousand years after the Big Bang, scientists say, light could not shine. The universe was too hot and violent—atoms smashing with such fury they formed a plasma-like soup. A subatomic sea.

As the universe expanded, matter cooled. Atoms collided, bonded, exploded, mixed. But all was still dark for about four hundred million years, according to NASA, until great gaseous clouds birthed the first stars. It would take another nine billion years of universal expansion— more turbulence than is fathomable—before our galaxy, with its hundred billion suns and at least eight billion earthlike worlds, began to shine.

Our sea has a savage birthing method too. At their origin, inside a tempest, waves are barely recognizable. They crash one on top of the other. No order. No respite. But these tempests send waves expanding in all directions. And as they gain distance from their raging origin, they sort themselves into organized patterns that will eventually break on sunny shores—perfect peeling lines that humans, dolphins, and seals love to ride.

Thus far in India, I'd felt I was in the most ferocious part of the storm. Scams, sickness, religious riots, heartache. But over the coming weeks in the Himalayas, I had the feeling that each day I was sailing farther from the hurricane. That all that pent-up, messy power was finding a tinge of order.

My first goal was to get out of my motel. But I had no money to upgrade, and the only alternative at the same price point doubled as a brothel. A few days later, however, while hiking again in the fields above town, I met Radhika, a mother out gathering wild herbs with her five-year-old twins, Bipham and Mehta.

There were no other people up in these highlands, and the twins sprinted toward me as if they knew me. As they got closer, they began leaping up to show me a small carved elephant statue they'd found buried in the grass. Radhika apologized for their pawing, but the twins were so cute, I didn't mind.

Radhika reminded me a bit of my own mother—

skinny and short, a gypsy head scarf wrapped around her wavy black hair like the scarves Mom used to wear when I was little. I thought of the Tibetan teaching that all beings, through beginningless time, have been our mother at one point or another.

Radhika spoke little English, but she managed to ask me where I was staying. I pointed to the cement block down the mountain and she muttered something to the twins in Hindi that made them chuckle.

"Come, come," she said. "You come my home. Please."

My first instinct was to make an excuse why I couldn't. But I *was* hoping to get away from the tourists so I could pretend I wasn't one. *It can't hurt to have a look,* I thought, and followed Radhika and the twins—who giggled the whole way—about a half mile down the trail to a wooden shack with a metal roof.

The house was about the size of your average lawn mower shed in the American suburbs. There was no toilet. The only means of bathing looked to be freezing well water and a coffee can. But the shanty overlooked a sloping meadow that was starting to bloom with purple and white flowers. Waking up to this wouldn't be bad. But when I ducked through the small front door, I didn't see where I could stay. Radhika, her rickshaw-driving husband, and the twins all slept on the floor in the single room that had a fire pit in the center for cooking.

"Thank you," I said. "But your family needs the space. I—"

Radhika shook her head and pulled back a curtain that ran along the wall, revealing a kitchen that wasn't tall enough to stand in and barely long enough to lie down in.

"You, here," Radhika said, and before I could refuse, she, Bipham, and Mehta began moving the kitchen cabinets into the main living space. They replaced all the kitchen cupboards with a single bed, made out of wood, that was about coffin-size.

OK, I thought, *I'll likely wake to some catch: "Now you take Bipham study America."* But since the front wall of the kitchen was lined with windows that overlooked the flowering meadow, sleeping here for one night seemed worth the risk.

I slept surprisingly well at Radhika's after hauling my pack from the motel. And in the morning, Bipham and Mehta woke me before sunrise with chai. After breakfast, Radhika showed me how to heat the well water with fire. The process only made a bucketful of scalding hot water, but standing in thirty-five degree air, shivering and dumping small canfuls of steaming water on each goose-bumped limb, then quickly soaping up and rinsing while singing, "fuck, fuck fuck it's fucking cold," turned out to be just the thing for feeling that I was in authentic India. Two nights turned into three, three into a week. A catch never came.

Guilty, I insisted I pay at least double what the motel charged—meaning two dollars—but Radhika said she couldn't accept more than one dollar per night.

"You very young," she said. "Must save money for wife."

Housing, check.

Next I had to figure out what I was doing up here. Besides finishing my undergraduate thesis, my whole excuse for being in India—so it wouldn't feel exclusively like chasing Sati—was to get credentials to get into Columbia Journalism School, which seemed, at the time, an official pass to adulthood and a writing career. At the start of this trip, I'd been reporting in politically hot areas so I could submit stories to American papers, but my only published article thus far was an op-ed in an Indian paper apologizing for George W. Bush.

The international irrelevance of McLeod was a strike against staying. But a few days after meeting Radhika, I was working at an expat café and overheard a middle-aged British woman saying, "Lobsong, you're confusing the lede." My ears perked up. That was journalism-speak! I eavesdropped through the conversation and interrupted at the first chance to see what they were up to.

"We're trying to keep this English-language magazine on the area afloat, but quite honestly, it's going to die if we don't find another English-speaking editor."

"I'm an English-speaking editor," I said, hoping she wouldn't ask about past experience.

"Well," the woman said, "when can you start?"

Job, check.

But it wasn't until I met Sonam that things really began to click.

Shortly after taking the volunteer editing job, I was strolling along Temple Road, looking up at prayer flags dangling from a veranda, when Sonam reached out his hand.

"Hello!" he said. "Welcome my home."

The voice startled me, and I nearly leapt into a sputtering rickshaw.

"Jesus!" I said, then looked up to see a young Tibetan monk laughing.

I dusted myself off, a little wary. Radhika had made me slightly more trusting of random friendliness, but before her offer, I'd been scammed at least a dozen times in this country. One time I'd entertained an overly friendly invitation to lunch and ended up at an awkward meal with a Nepali father asking me to marry one of his five daughters.

But Sonam had a trustworthy face: simultaneously round and defined, high cheekbones perking up shiny black eyes. I liked him straightaway. We went through the usual foreigner discussion.

"Where from?"

"California."

"Ahhhh, nice!"

I figured it couldn't hurt to accept his invitation to tour the monastery and have dinner.

The monastery was just a few cement rooms for eating, meditating, and studying. But it was adorned with silk mandala paintings and intricate statues formed from brightly dyed yak butter. Tibetan and Sanskrit texts with weathered spines covered some of the walls.

We ate mung beans and rice with the other monks in silence. Then, after dinner, Sonam brought me to the flat cement roof—rusted rebar still popping out from the cinder blocks. Here, he made his pitch.

Sonam was searching for a tutor to help with conversational English. He hoped to teach other monks and was wondering if I could chat with him on occasion. In exchange, he'd teach me Tibetan or, if I wanted, how to make yak-butter statues.

I didn't see yak-butter sculpting in my future. But my thesis compared Buddhist and Hindu sects and was in need of some interviews. If Sonam would be my interviewee, I said, I'd meet with him for an hour per day of English.

"Wah!" Sonam said. "Soooo happy!"

I was still a wreck. I often woke up wanting to beat my head against the granite. I still hoped every moment that Sati would email and tell me she'd seen the light and wanted to run away to Tahiti together. But I considered myself on an upswing from breakup hell. I also had a sense of purpose: two jobs—albeit unpaid. And I wanted to keep them.

So, at our first tutoring session the next day, I met Sonam on the monastery roof, bringing a few English grammar books I'd picked up at a used bookstore. I was feeling proud of myself for being organized. But not long after beginning a conversational lesson, Sonam looked a bit bored. He told me what he loved most was singing.

"Chanting?" I asked.

"Ya, ya, chant good," Sonam said, "but Bollywood good too. If no monk, I tink maybe, how you say, star singing?"

"A rock star?"

"No, no. Not rock. Star, you know star?"

I was about to explain what rock star meant. But Sonam was already breaking into a Hindi dance routine from the Bollywood epic *Devdas*. He put his hand to his heart as he sung and pointed at the heavens.

Sonam's voice wasn't great. And monkhood hadn't exactly given him solid dance moves. But after he finished his jig, I told Sonam I played a little guitar. His eyes sparked.

"I come back, I come back!" he said.

A few minutes later, Sonam returned carrying an acoustic guitar. Canadian tourists had recently stayed at the monastery, he said, and hadn't been able to pay their room fees. Feeling bad, they'd offered the monks the guitar.

Judging from its looks, the Canadians had gotten off easy. Even tuned up, the guitar sounded like a wet barrel with strings. But a beat-up guitar was slightly better than no guitar. And English tutoring became a jam.

I tried to explain the meaning behind Dylan, the Beatles, and Petty, which I generally did poorly because I often had no clue of the meanings myself. That said, "Let It Be" became a quick favorite when I explained it in terms of nonattachment. Nothing could compare to Sonam's exuberance, though, when we got to John Denver's "Take Me Home, Country Roads."

"*Wah! Wah!* Dis beautiful song!" Sonam beamed. "Dis what feel every day! Dis Tibet many many missing. Every day sing my homeland far away!"

I got a lump in my throat. You couldn't walk down the street in McLeod without reading some human rights pamphlet about Buddhist monks and nuns being tortured, kidnapped, or killed by Chinese security. Gedhun Choekyi Nyima, the young boy who had been chosen as the reincarnation of the Panchen Lama—the most holy Tibetan figure after the Dalai Lama—had been kidnapped and activists were constantly parading the boy's adorable face around town. I'd chatted with other monks and nuns since arriving, and their easygoing manner made you forget they'd lost anything at all. But Sonam's connection with "Country Roads" made me remember that even the monastics—despite their daily equanimity training—were in constant mourning and trauma recovery.

★ ★ ★

From then on, Sonam and I sang "Country Roads" every class, usually a minimum of four times. Only instead of "almost heaven, West Virginia," we sang "almost heaven, West Tibet." Every single time, Sonam got misty-eyed midchorus. Once he cried.

He didn't seem to want to talk about the tears though. Didn't seem to want to burden me. But after four or five weeks of tutoring, Sonam and I began hanging out beyond English class. We'd cook dinner together or go walking in the hills. The details gradually became clear.

When Sonam was eleven, a Nepali man had come through his tiny village in Tibet. The man wanted to see if anyone in Sonam's family would go with him on a trek to India to see the Dalai Lama. Sonam's whole family declined— except Sonam. He knew even then that he wanted to be a monk. And he was so insistent, his family agreed to let him go, asking only that Sonam return to see them as soon as he could.

With no compass or map, Sonam and the Nepali man took such an arduous route they had to eat grass to stay alive. Sonam needed a year of medical care in Nepal to nurse him back from malnutrition. But he finally made it to India where he did ordain under the Dalai Lama—a moment that he described as "best day my life!"

Fifteen years later, when I met Sonam, he still loved being a monk. But he loved his family too. Chinese security had increased since he'd left Tibet. With no mail or telephone service to his village, he hadn't even been able to write, much less visit. He didn't know if they were alive and presumably they didn't know the same about him. Often he dreamt about them, worrying they'd been imprisoned or worse.

Once I knew Sonam's full story, I told him bits about my own life, including the Sati tragedy, and we became close.

"You best friend, Ja-ma," Sonam started saying. "I tink one day, you me Tibet going. See family. You bring wife, baby."

"Sonam," I said, "I don't even have a girlfriend anymore."

"Soon, soon," Sonam laughed.

I loved the idea of going to Tibet with Sonam and couldn't help imagining Sati as the wife Sonam was prophesying about. But the fantasy seemed far-fetched.

"You never know," I usually shrugged, not wanting to let either of us get carried away. But as if we already had tickets, Sonam would often launch into the details he hoped to show me: how his house sat alone on a remote hillside, nothing else for miles and miles around ("dis big big sky—you sing, 'waaaaaah!' nobody hear"), how he and his older brother would play pranks on each other ("dis Tibet game, tricky tricky"), about his mother's homemade cheese and his father's folk religion ("dis mountain-people religion, good religion, Buddhism same same").

Sonam's eyes often moistened when talking about his

family. But after just a few weeks of knowing him, I remember thinking Sonam was, without question, the happiest person I'd ever met.

"Dis morning, I bery happy," he would say while he made us thick Tibetan chai with milk.

"Dis night, I bery happy," he would say in the evening as we cooked dinner.

"Dis *puja* make me bery bery happy," he'd say when we did Tibetan chanting.

Quite literally, Sonam said he was "bery bery happy" at least twenty times a day.

At first I wondered if it was all an act. Sonam may not have seen *Seven Years in Tibet*, but he'd seen enough stressed-out tourists to know how the roles broke down. He was the happy monk and had to woo me, the miserable Westerner burdened by my lust for wealth, into simplicity and grace. But after weeks and then months of "so happy this, so happy that," I realized it wasn't what Sonam was saying that made him convincing. It was that I felt happier and lighter whenever I was around him. And since I was still tortured fairly regularly by dreams of Sati's parents inviting Jyanth for afternoon tea, this was an improvement.

But I often wondered how Sonam maintained his contentment while also clearly grieving. I felt that I had two settings: upbeat and joyful—usually due to the future feeling bright—or guilt and despair—because the future seemed difficult. These settings were more like rivals, dark and light, than parts of myself that could live in harmony.

I'll never know the exact functioning of Sonam's psychology, only what I perceived through my own projections and needs. But one spring morning, I thought I got a clear glimpse.

Sonam had invited me with him to make offerings to Tibetan hermits who live high above McLeod deepening their meditation and preparing for death. We'd brought gallons of milk, some vegetables, prayer flags, and dried herbs to burn as an offering to the Buddhas and bodhisattvas. Sonam was ecstatic as we hiked.

"Today, I bery bery happy. Dis going big mountain. Dis big lama see. Dis lama many many meditation."

Walking up the narrow path, we sang our usual "Country Roads" along with some Tibetan folk songs. We laughed as I botched the Tibetan lyrics and he botched the English ones. But when we passed the snow line, Sonam knelt down and scooped snow in his palms, rubbing it between his fingers, watching it melt.

"Dis snow many many sad," he said. "Tibet snow bery same same. Dis longtime no see."

Sonam stared at the snow for a while in silence. And since I'd earned this new best-friend slot, I put my hand on his shoulder. "I'm sorry," I said. "I'm sorry you can't go home, Sonam."

I expected Sonam to take the opportunity to talk more about Tibet. He seemed to be getting more used to this Western approach I'd introduced him to—constant emotional venting. But instead, he looked at my concerned expression, smiled wide, and said something I will never forget:

"Ja-ma, you funny. Dis bery sad no problem."

4

without a hat
a winter rain falls on me
so what

—MATSUO BASHO

came to depend on Sonam's jovial moods more than I knew. So when he had to go to South India for a couple of weeks to help a sick teacher, I found myself hiking the trail toward the hermits almost every day, humming our usual tunes.

One morning, early enough that there were still frozen puddles thawing on the trail, I stopped at a boulder that had been split in two by a pine root. The massive stone sat alone in the path, and it struck me because I didn't want it whole.

The stone was just cracked. And in its cracked state, it was as beautiful as any rock—even more so. And maybe this was what the sages were getting at. Cracked, shiny, or beaten to dust, we just are, and when all the mental gymnastics are removed, that's enough.

The more I hiked the trail alone, the more I sensed that. Up here, there wasn't as much need for any special concentration techniques or yogas. The mind just settled into the blue pines, spruce, and fir stands. As it did, the memory patterns of Sati and me—the ones I'd convinced myself were proof of our soul mate status—became more porous.

But a day does not consist of pacing a trail. In town, my mind would quickly shift back to striving mode. I was putting a lot of pressure on myself to be productive in writing. Often I'd work late into the night, lose too much sleep, and find myself in a twisted state of anxiety. I worried I'd never amount to anything, that I'd screwed up my life by leaving Sati the first time, that I'd screw up again and again forever.

Some part of me knew this was in my head. But this knowledge made me even more frustrated because I should, I thought, know better. Why couldn't I accept my cracked self like the cracked stone?

The Dalai Lama had begun his two-week teaching at his monastery on Temple Road. In all Buddhist schools, it's said there are eighty-four thousand dharma doors, which is basically another way of saying there are infinite paths to enlightenment. But Tibetan Buddhist schools seem to emphasize the variety more than other sects. Tibetans often note that a true master, a true bodhisattva, is a compassionate doctor. Enlightenment is the simplest thing imaginable, goes the saying, but our mental diseases are complex. A good teacher is there to deliver custom meds.

The Dalai Lama comes from the epitome of the scholarly door. It's a variation of Vajrayana—a blending of strands of tantric yoga and Mahayana Buddhism—called *Gelugpa* in which monks get the equivalent of multiple PhDs in philosophy. In Gelugpa, quite the opposite of Zen at least in preliminary practice, it's only when this philosophical foundation has been laid, and lengthy ritualistic purifications completed, that true meditation begins. And during the Dalai Lama's two-week talks, he speaks for eight hours straight every day (no teleprompter, no notes).

I had great respect for Gelugpa, which Sonam was a part of. But I overthought things to begin with. One hundred and twelve hours straight of Tibetan metaphysics, I had a hunch, was not my dharma door.

That said, I loved to go to the teachings in the mornings to take in the scene: Nepali and Tibetan pilgrims—some of whom had hiked hundreds of miles making full-body prostrations to the Buddhas with each step—kneeling alongside Western psychologists, Australian surfers with neck tattoos, ascetic yogis in white dhotis, and thousands of maroon-robed monks and nuns all sipping their salty butter tea.

One afternoon when Sonam was still away, I was sitting on the outskirts of this assembly when Vella sidled up beside me.

"Howdy, stranger," she said.

The voice startled me, and I jumped, disturbing some nearby meditators.

"Sorry," I whispered. But then I turned and saw her.

"Vella!" I said, whispering a shout. "What! What are you doing here? I didn't know you were in India!"

"I live here," she said. "What the hell are you doing here?"

She laughed and gave me a friendly punch in the gut.

Vella was a fast-talking, bald-headed New Yorker I'd done a yoga-teacher training with a few years earlier. The training was at an Orthodox ashram led by the great Indian yogi Baba Hari Dass. And at the time, Vella had just been testing the whole yoga scene. Now she looked to have drunk the Kool-Aid: sandalwood *malas* wrapped around her wrists, a Tibetan shawl draped over her shoulders, the standard red string around the neck that meant you'd been blessed by a high lama.

I teased her about her new look—"No Sanskrit tattoos yet?"—but Vella looked fantastic. Her dark eyes had that shimmer of depth and true health. Her smile beamed. Even her skin was radiant. But she hadn't lost her wit.

"You look amazing," I said.

"Thanks," she said. "You look awful."

I rolled my eyes.

"Tough times," I said.

"Ladies?"

"What other force could be so destructive?"

(Vella was gay, which made me feel like she could relate to my problem even more.)

"You need tea," she said.

* * *

We wove around a crowd of prostrating pilgrims, then descended the stairs to a small tea house, part of the monastery, that smelled like fresh noodles and cardamom. Over dumplings and chai, Vella summarized her story of the last three years. She'd thought she was going to the yoga-teacher training to get some work-life balance from her stressful finance career. But yoga had introduced her to meditation, meditation to Tibetan Buddhism, "and now pretty much all I do is follow lamas around Asia," she said. "Yep, full-time junkie. No job. No relationship. Nothing. And, Jaimal, I am so, so, so happy."

I believed Vella. Her face said it all. And as I listened, I had the peculiar sense of looking at the me that could have been.

About three years earlier, when we'd done our yoga training, Vella had been the one in class asking questions like, "How do we find time to do yoga and meditate every day? I mean, I work *hard*." Or, "Is it OK to drink coffee before and after yoga?"

Meanwhile, I had ended up at the training to find a way to readjust into the world after living in the Ch'an monastery. I felt grateful I didn't even comprehend Vella's stress. But three years later, here I was hustling to get credentials for a journalism career and to chase Sati. And though I was doing a bit better since meeting Sonam, on balance, I still felt fairly awful. According to Vella, I also looked half-dead. Vella had done the opposite, and she looked like she'd been drinking from the same grail as our old guru Baba Hari Dass. In his nineties as I write this, the man still looks like he should be modeling for anti-wrinkle cream ads.

I told Vella about Sati, and refreshingly, she didn't give advice.

"Relationships," she shrugged. "You need to go on retreat. Now."

I didn't see Vella after that brief tea. She was shipping off to be a translator for a lama in Nepal. But much of my family hails from New York, and something about Vella's hit of spiritual Brooklyn made me trust her. The very next day, I went on retreat.

The Vipassana meditation center I went to was run out of a yurt in a smaller town above McLeod called Bhagsunath. It was as basic as it gets: dirt floors, a single image of the Buddha on a wooden table, old military-style canvas tents with cots to sleep on.

Based on the Buddhist system of *dana* (giving), the retreat center also didn't charge a dime for food or lodging, which helped me breathe easier the minute I walked in. The funds from my student loans were so low the one-dollar-per-night charge at Radhika's was starting to make a dent.

Vipassana—which means "insight" in Pali—is a system of meditation built on the Buddha's teachings in the *Satipatthana Sutta*, a text from which the notion of mindfulness seems to have originated. The opening lines summarize the thrust:

A monk, having gone to the forest, to the foot of a tree or to an empty place, sits down with his legs crossed, keeps his body erect and his mindfulness alert. Ever mindful he breathes in, mindful he breathes out. Breathing in a long breath, he knows, "I am breathing in a long breath"; breathing out a long breath, he knows, "I am breathing out a long breath"; breathing in a short breath, he knows, "I am breathing in a short breath"; breathing out a short breath, he knows, "I am breathing out a short breath."

In other words, you witness what's in front of you—breath, sensation, thoughts, feelings—without trying to change what's in front of you. That sounds almost ridiculously easy, so easy it would be pointless to mention. But scientists now know that doing this simple act every day has an incredible number of great side effects: it increases immune function, decreases pain and inflammation, increases positive emotion, decreases depression, and on and on. Doctors are now prescribing mindfulness for everything from back pain to postpartum depression. But for early Buddhists the point was not only getting better grades, fewer colds, and feeling a little happier. It was to actually *end suffering*—like, for good. Thoughts create our reality, went the thinking, and suffering is an experience in the mind. Master your thoughts—or simply let them be without constant reactions and identification—and you master reality. You master being.

★ ★ ★

I liked Vipassana and the *Theravada* school of Buddhism it arose out of. This early sect of Buddhism laid the foundation of all Buddhist meditation. But *Theravada*—which means "way of the ancients" and thrives especially in places like Thailand, Burma, and Cambodia—tends to be slightly more relaxed than that hard-core Chinese approach I'd been trained in. Chinese culture prides itself on the ability to endure hardship, and I had a wee chip on my shoulder as I strolled into this mountain yurt. The schedule called for eight hours of meditation per day, and sitting practice finished at 9:00 p.m. This is a lot. But compared to our old Ch'an schedule, it was like running a half marathon instead of the full twenty-six.

I'd forgotten, however, that when you've been running around in the bustle of everyday life—movies, emails, friends, family, music for distractions—stopping those distractions cold turkey is shocking. Suddenly you're alone in a strange place—your mind. For what seems like way, way too long.

The moment the retreat bell dinged, my mind came up with infinite excuses about why I should be *anywhere* but alone with it in a yurt at eight thousand feet in India.

"I should be writing!" I told myself on day one. "I'll never get into grad school now! Sati will have been right to leave me—a failure."

On day two, my Ch'an ego took the wheel again: "These teachers are weak. I should be in China, not India."

On day three, I developed a crush on a United Nations

worker who was volunteering at a nearby refugee camp, and I spent the entire day fantasizing about how I might approach her when we were allowed to talk again. Soon I'd even played out a passionate romance and happy life together—two children, a cottage in Bali, a successful crusade against world hunger.

But on day four, I abandoned this fantasy and began stewing about the teacher, an elderly Indian man, for telling me not to do yoga during the retreat.

"Simply do the meditation," he said. "The practice is all you need."

I smiled, but was thinking, *And all you need to do is remember we're in the middle of the fucking Himalayas! I think a little yoga is OK.* (I was carrying around a lot of anger.)

By day five, I began to settle into the practice and felt just on the cusp of some good old-fashioned retreat peace. But when the pitch and chop of the mind begin to settle, when you sink into the still depths, you occasionally find the tentacled creatures that live down there.

On day six, I got hit with a memory of Sati and me in Hawaii. It was a simple image. Just us with our feet in a tide pool near Hilo, giggling and about to go for a snorkel. She was wearing a gold one-piece bathing suit and was joking about jellyfish and how locals had told her to pee on herself if one stung her.

It wasn't much. But for whatever reason, surrounded by a thick crowd of mindful breathers, each sorting through their infinite psychological knots, I began to convulse. I began to sob.

I restrained myself enough not to sob for the rest of the hour—wasn't I supposed to be a zen warrior here?—but when the bell rang, I ran out to my tent, plunged my head in my pillow, and bawled like I had never bawled before. I cried for an hour straight, a sort of wheezing tantrum that I didn't even think was possible anymore.

At the end, I felt better and assumed that it was over.

"Minor technical difficulty," I tried to say with subtle glances to my neighbors, especially the United Nations woman.

But during the next sit, it happened again.

Then again.

Then again.

Meditate. Cry. Meditate. Scream and punch pillow. Meditate. Weep until donkey grunts and hiccups set in.

Silent retreat had become weeping retreat.

In those early Ch'an retreats, I'd had this vague notion that meditation was all about cutting off emotion with razor-sharp focus—about getting tough on pain, which was ultimately a mental illusion. And before meeting Sonam, I would have forced myself to stop crying. I would have sucked it up and soldiered on. But in the midst of my sobbing, hokey as it may sound, I felt as if Sonam was coaching me from the sidelines: "Ja-ma, look! Dis bery sad, noooo problem. Big sad berrrry OK!"

So I tried to follow my coach. I tried to just let the sadness be. And it was interesting. Once I stopped being angry at myself for not being enlightened, for being a human with feelings, the crying and sobbing and pounding ceased to be so bad. I wouldn't have minded if they left and never came back, but still, while bleating and hiccuping, if I surrendered, the wave of emotion became a surge more akin to unrestrained laughter than to depression. It was actually strangely pleasant.

And the more the tears were allowed to flow, the more the sobbing shifted away from Sati. There I'd be, head in pillow, but I was also an eleven-year-old boy watching Mom collapse by the sink as Pa said he was leaving the marriage. I was a six-year-old at a new kindergarten, terrified to speak to the other kids who looked so easy and carefree. I was a fifteen-year-old getting high and caught in another stupid lie that was hurting someone I loved.

I'd never cried about any of it. I'd taken up the torch of our military family and spent my whole life soldiering through grief, flipping the bird at sadness as if it was weakness. But Sonam had revealed a truth so obvious it was the easiest to miss: you couldn't run away from sadness any more than a river can run uphill.

Life was sad. Really sad. Loss. Sickness. Cruelty. Death. There was no way around it. But sadness, when it was allowed to be itself, was strangely not sad. Sadness was just sadness. Tears just salt water.

5

When you begin to question your dream, awakening will not be far away.

—SRI NISARGADATTA MAHARAJ

Over these sea-pastures, wide-rolling watery prairies and Potters' Fields of all four continents, the waves should rise and fall; for here, millions of mixed shades and shadows, drowned dreams, somnambulisms, reveries; all that we call lives and souls, lie dreaming, dreaming still.

—HERMAN MELVILLE, MARDI

ema Chodron, an American nun in the Tibetan Buddhist tradition, tells a story about Milarepa, one of the most revered Tibetan sages, who lived during the twelfth century. One night, Milarepa came back to his meditation cave and found a horde of demons.

"He had the sense that they were just a projection of his own mind," Chodron writes, "all the unwanted parts of himself." But he still didn't know how to get rid of them.

At this point, Milarepa had been at this spiritual practice stuff for a while. He had a few tools. So he tried lecturing the demons on the dharma, the Buddhist teachings. No luck. Milarepa raged at them. They laughed. Finally, he gave up and said, "Looks like you're not going anywhere and I'm not either, so let's just live here together."

Then, as if Milarepa had spoiled the demons' fun, all of them left—all but one really nasty one with horrible fangs. And "we all know that one," Chodron writes. "Sometimes we have lots of them like that. Sometimes we feel that's all we've got."

With this demon, Milarepa knew he'd have to be smart. So he walked up and stood face-to-face with it, feeling its hot breath. Then he promptly stuck his head into the demon's mouth. That demon then left too.

When I lived at the monastery, I occasionally practiced with a group of monks in the Thai Forest tradition too. Some of these monks were British, and though monks don't traditionally eat after noon, these British guys not surprisingly had found a loophole for afternoon tea. So, one afternoon over chocolate and Earl Grey, they told a story about a pilgrimage they'd been on through India together. While they were heading to Delhi, bandits hijacked the bus and began stealing the passengers' wallets at knifepoint. Thai Forest monks never touch money. They beg for all their food. And when the bandits got to these orange-robed bald men, some of the novice monks were afraid. But one of the elder monks walked directly up to a robber, pointed at the knife, and then, as if in an episode of *Game of Thrones*, he bared his neck, daring the man to slice.

The robbers fled.

I was thinking of both of these stories as the crying tapered off on day seven. My neighbors looked relieved I was no longer gagging. And that night I had a dream.

The dream began without images, just blackness. Just sensation. Someone or something was scratching in my chest, behind the breastplate, rummaging through me with a steel comb, a pine branch, chicken wire.

There were mutterings in a language that I couldn't understand. So I bolted up in bed. And there, kneeling at my bedside, was an old Tibetan man with frail features and silver hair. He smiled and nodded, then reached his hand into my chest *Indiana Jones and the Temple of Doom*–style. He twisted his hand just so, casually removed a few black stones from my heart, then tossed the stones aside as if he were gutting a fish.

You'd think I would have screamed or spoken up. But there was something ordinary about this visit—something half expected. Did I know this man?

He removed more black stones. Then he closed his eyes, as if to pray. I closed my eyes too. But when my dream eyes shut, I woke up. I was in the same tent. There was no Tibetan man. It was morning.

★ ★ ★

Meditation practice, like any practice, has a cumulative nature. But something important did shift after that dream. And for the final few days of retreat, I felt at ease—myself with nothing added—a state that seemed like the most normal thing imaginable and also the most precious gift.

How to explain? I felt like a patient who'd been diagnosed with a terminal illness and given the medicine, but then, in a strange bout of amnesia, had forgotten to take it. I was ecstatic to have remembered; when the ten days of silence ended, I turned right around and did another ten days of silence at the Tibetan retreat center next door. (Thank you, Vella!)

I won't bore you with the details of more silence, but the next retreat was equally fruitful. And walking down to McLeod from Bhagsunath with mischievous rhesus monkeys leaping above me in the pines, I wanted to bow to everything for this practice, a practice that truly did dispel suffering. And not by blind faith. By simple awareness of what's here *now*, always, moment by moment, breath by breath.

I wondered if this was the fresh, happy mind Sonam woke with every morning, and when I found him chopping cabbage in his single room off the monastery, I felt I was seeing my real brother. I tiptoed under the prayer flags that hung from his front door, trying to sneak up and surprise him. But spoiling my fun, Sonam turned casually as though he'd known I was there all along. "Wah!" he said. "Ja-ma. Dis good meditation. I many many tinking you on mountain. I pray you every day."

I thanked Sonam for the good wishes, and after some chitchat about his trip south, I couldn't help telling him about the dream. Sonam nodded while continuing to chop cabbage.

"Ya, ya!" he said as if we were discussing dinner ingredients. "I tink maybe you see my old teacher. He die. I pray him help you."

Now. Had this dream happened at any other time or place, I would have either blown this comment off as folk superstition or rattled Sonam by the shoulders and insisted he explain every detail. (*Let's compare notes! Did he have a little goatee and a mole under his left eye?*) But after several months in these mountains, I'd grown a bit more comfortable with the common Tibetan worldview. And for Tibetans, the borders between dream states and what we call reality are not *necessarily* there. Waking life is seen as produced by the collective mind just as dreaming is produced by our thoughts. Many Tibetans, in fact, practice dream yoga, the cultivation of directed lucid dreaming, in which sleep becomes another chance for subtle yogic practices.

The dream realm, which is said to mirror the space between lives, is thought to prepare a yogi for death. So the idea that you'd be able to pray to a deceased teacher and then have that teacher show up in a dream is as commonplace as being able to ask your friend to buy you broccoli at the market.

I wasn't at the point of seeing dream and reality as one. But after twenty days of silence, my waking state did seem more pleasantly dreamlike. Circumstances had not changed. Sati was still far away. I still had a very long the-sis to write. I hadn't gotten into grad school or published anything (save an article on chai in that local magazine, which, just as I'd feared, nobody read). But all of this was a few measly brushstrokes on a canvas as large as space itself.

Maybe Sati and I would someday be together. Most likely not. Maybe I'd get into school. Maybe I'd be a bum. But none of it would make or break this joy I'd stumbled on again—a gem I'd had all along but had forgotten when I'd buried it beneath possessiveness, fear, and heedlessness. It was all so plain wonderful—life. Why wasn't everyone jumping for joy about this fact that now seemed so blatant: Happiness and freedom are already ours without accumulating anything new. They're ours if we strip back the layers of thought and sense the original spaciousness of our minds.

Anyhow, the very next day Sonam said he was going to make offerings to the hermits again, and I jumped at the chance to come along. The first time we'd made the journey, the hermit we'd been looking for wasn't in his hut. This time I hoped would be different.

"I bery happy," Sonam said as we climbed the now-familiar trail. "I tink we Tibet going togeder soon. See family! My family so happy you, make many many momo!"

Usually, this was my cue to shrug and smile. But *momos*, Tibetan dumplings, are my favorite Tibetan food, and on retreat I'd spent many hours daydreaming of going to Tibet with Sonam. Maybe even writing about the journey.

I asked Sonam if he thought we could sneak into Tibet to see his family. "No, no, no, too danger danger," he said. "Many monk, dis Tibet going, no coming back. Dis many prison."

We changed the subject. But the question clearly got Sonam thinking because he soon began telling stories of Tibetans who had bribed their way through security guards to safely return home. It took me a while to understand what he was cooking up, but I soon realized Sonam was saying he wanted to come to America with me where he thought he could get a job in a Tibetan restaurant. From there, he thought he could earn enough money to come back to India and bribe his way into Tibet. I could help him get to the US, he said.

"You bery good, Ja-ma. For you, dis visa no problem."

I had a sinking feeling, my first inkling of postretreat anxiety. I knew this was a terrible plan. Getting the US visa alone would be next to impossible; getting a job in the US would be equally hard; saving money while living in the US would be even harder; and getting the Chinese visa (legally or illegally) would be nothing short of a miracle. But Sonam was excited in a way I hadn't yet seen.

"Dis good plan! Dis good plan!" he repeated. "You help me?"

Again, had this been any other time or place, I think I would have reasoned my way through. But today I was thinking that Sonam had just sent his dead teacher to heal my broken heart in a dream. Maybe anything was possible. I put my arm around Sonam.

"Of course," I said. "This good plan."

We reached the huts in the afternoon and went straight for one that was made of weathered wood, torn blue plastic tarps, sheet metal, and mud. Sonam knew this hermit well.

"Dis lama mind many many color, bery beautiful."

We knocked at the metal door, and a tall round-faced lama opened it right away.

"*Tashi delek!*" the lama said, using the traditional greeting that literally means "auspicious." Then the lama immediately started laughing.

"How strange," he said to Sonam in Tibetan. "Today I made lunch for three!"

It seemed as if we were entering a bad episode of *Kung Fu: The Legend Continues.* ("Ah, I've been expecting you.") But it was true. The lama had made lunch for three: three servings of cabbage and rice.

While we ate, Sonam and the lama spoke in Tibetan, occasionally translating for me. How was the lama's health? Was he getting enough food? Sonam then told the lama about his plans to go to America. I was almost positive the hermit would warn Sonam away from this complicated scheme.

But the lama began nodding and laughing. He looked a little too pleased.

"What's he saying?" I asked.

"He say plan bery good," said Sonam.

I raised my eyebrows and forced a smile.

"Great," I said.

At the end of the meal, the lama wrapped my hands tightly in his and muttered for what seemed like a few minutes. I thought he might be telling me something important about my path and future, something like: *You're the one we've been waiting for. Sonam and you will change the earth forever!* Sonam later translated what he said as: "Thank you for helping Sonam. You're a good person."

Still, it was a memorable moment. I'd read studies that Tibetan monks, when reflecting on compassion, could produce twenty times the amount of gamma-wave activity that ordinary people could, but experiencing that compassion was very different from seeing it on a graph. While gripping my hands, the lama looked into my eyes as if he was going to cry. I remember my whole body quivering. I remember knowing without the slightest doubt that all the prayers these monks recite every day—"May all beings find peace, and the causes of peace; may all beings find happiness and the causes of happiness"—work to transform their hearts.

6

My mind is like the autumn moon
shining clean and clear in the green pool.
No, that's not a good comparison.
Tell me, how should I explain?

—HAN SHAN

Sonam and I walked down the hill, singing the same old songs, and Sonam said: "I so bery happy. We going America. Dis big building, bery clean. Dis many many work. Tibet going—see family. My family saying, 'Wah wah, Sonam!' Dis many many hugging hugging. 'Wah! Wah! Sonam! Sonam!'"

Seeing Sonam beam, I couldn't help but feel that we'd done right. Yes, this was insane. But my anxiety from the hut was already fading into the forest. And what if the plan really could work? I mean, a high lama had blessed our idea. Maybe I'd actually be flying home with my new best friend. Maybe everything would work perfectly.

Everything did seem kind of perfect for a while. Over the next month, I maintained a supercharged meditation and writing regimen, finished my thesis, and still had time to volunteer at the magazine. The frustration about Sati was gone—well, just about, which was better than I'd dreamed possible at the start of this trip. And, of course, the moment I was feeling that I didn't need any relationship at all, Sati's long-awaited email arrived.

"I have some time to come and visit!" she wrote. "Any chance I can catch you before you leave?"

"With Jyanth?" I wrote.

"We broke up," she replied.

I still wasn't sure Sati would actually come. Feeling about 73 percent unattached to the outcome, I told her I'd love to see her, and then Sonam and I got down to business on our plan.

Puzzle pieces were falling into place too. Tara, a Human Rights Watch fellow, and Tyler, a Canadian traveler, volunteered to help our cause. Previously, Tyler had been studying international law while teaching break dancing to Bollywood stars. And having a human rights star and a lawyer-to-be—one who could do the robot—made us feel legit.

Every night we performed *pujas*—ceremonial offerings and chants—which Sonam said would clear away all karmic obstructions to our success. Word spread around McLeod that Sonam was going home with me, and I occasionally saw other monks in town give me the thumbs-up.

I still had nagging doubts. Of course I did. But with Sonam's ceaseless optimism and Tyler's and Tara's brains, each doubt that raised its voice became an unruly child that I sent to time-out.

"Dis every night dreaming America," Sonam said often.

What could stand in our way?

The day finally came when Sonam and I took our eighty-six-page visa application on the bus to Delhi. Tyler, Tara, and a small parade of monks from Sonam's monastery accompanied us to the bus stop, and one senior monk even wore an American flag T-shirt.

We waved to them through the windows, hearts full of optimism. But an hour into the bumpy ride——on a road on which there were no guardrails, and many rusted cars lay at the base of massive cliffs——our bus screeched to an uncomfortable halt inches from the edge.

Locals are used to this sort of thing happening. So as we all hobbled off the bus and saw that a tire had nearly fallen off, I seemed to be the only one who thought we'd just evaded death. Nobody, including Sonam, seemed bothered when the bus driver and some local mechanics began removing one bolt from each of the other three remaining tires in order to repair the fourth.

I considered trying to hitchhike back to McLeod to splurge for a taxi. But Sonam said, "Dis OK, Ja-ma, many many happen."

I wanted to remind Sonam that "many many people die." But I thought of a Tibetan saying: "If you lose your leg, be grateful you still have your head." I sighed and got back on the bus. If we died, at least I'd die with Sonam.

We made it to Delhi—land of stadium-size slums next to air-conditioned Starbucks—and, just like my last visit, it was about 112 degrees. Delhi still smelled of diesel, laundry detergent, burning trash, and a combination of spices I couldn't place, which struck me as more nauseating than usual because the sixteen-hour bus ride had left me ill. I was officially edgy and agitated for the first time since the retreat. I then added frustration to this as I realized my seemingly bulletproof retreat love was just another passing state. And as the icing on the cake, when we arrived at our shanty motel, I reached into my backpack pocket and found my passport had been stolen from my backpack while we'd been napping on the bus.

"Noooooo!" I whined, wilting in the hot lobby. "Come on!"

I hated Delhi. I really hated Delhi.

"Ja-ma," Sonam said, "dis passport easy replace. US embassy already going."

"You're right," I said. I closed my eyes, said a few silent motherfuckers, smiled through gritted teeth, and then tried to switch back to pleasant mantras.

I kept these going at the motel for a little while, sort of proud of myself for a decent mental recovery. But I still had to make a police report to get my new passport. And when I crossed town—this time without Sonam, who also needed to run errands—to report the theft, a gang of police officers smoking cigarettes outside the station tried to sell me cocaine.

"Come, come, American!" they guffawed. "Cocaine, cocaine. Good cocaine. You like cocaine, boss?"

Having visions of entrapment schemes, I decided to report my passport lost. And walking past a slum on my way back to the motel—throat dry, drenched in sweat—I gave a few rupees to some homeless kids and began to wonder if Delhi might be a whirlpool portal to hell. In a split second, the city could suck you under to the lowest level of the inferno. Suddenly you'd be in an Indian prison for buying cocaine you hadn't ever seen, and you would do anything, *anything* to get out.

No, no, I told myself. *Get it together, Yogis. It's the heat. It's just the heat.*

I got back to the motel and suggested Sonam and I have *rava dosas* for dinner, a favorite dish that was impossible to find in McLeod. Sonam agreed. And after an evening meditation, the temperature had dropped to a tolerable ninety-two. Walking through a beautiful historical quarter, sampling dosas and drinking sweet lassi, convinced me that Delhi was not a whirlpool to hell. I was back.

We slept soundly, doing one final puja before bed. But when we finally arrived at the embassy the next day and the line to get our application review was six hours long and full of people who had been previously rejected even though they had more legitimate reasons than us—one young woman had been accepted to Yale—I was beginning to wonder, again, if I should have warned Sonam against all of this. Had I been an irresponsible friend? Had meditation made me go nuts?

No, not again. We'd come so far. And we believed! We'd chanted!

So when we finally got to the window, whispering mantras, and the American embassy worker glanced at our huge packet of official papers with official stamps from the Dalai Lama's own office, he gave the packet one more official stamp without even looking at our faces: REJECTED.

The next twenty-four hours are blurry. I think I blocked them out. Sonam said he wanted some time alone at the motel. All I remember is wandering zombielike between air-conditioned shops, haggling for a few last gifts for my family, avoiding the lepers and beggars, wishing we'd never come.

I also remember we went to a terrible restaurant that night, and Sonam, for the first time since I'd known him, ate meat. It seemed that after all those pujas, the rejection had shaken his faith.

"Today I bery sad," he said. "I sorry, Ja-ma. Bery sorry. Dis plan no good."

That night, I felt angry. Angry at the cruel universe. Angry at myself. Angry at the Buddhas and God. Spinning prayer wheels and visualizing bodhisattvas was lovely in the Himalayas. But down here, compassion suffocated in the dust and heat and open sewage. Maybe you were better off never coming down the mountain at all. Maybe you were better off escaping as far as possible from refugees, from poverty, from corruption, from disease. The world was rotting and nothing could be done. We went to bed silently, without our normal chants. I dreamt restless dreams of war.

The next day, Sonam was up early doing his ceremony before the sun rose. When I heard him, I rolled over and had that feeling of not knowing which city I was waking up in. When I remembered, I realized I needed to get out of this whole country—now, maybe today. I couldn't handle another sixteen-hour bus ride, another shower with a coffee can, another hole-in-the-ground toilet. I wanted fast internet. *Saturday Night Live.* Toilet paper.

I expected Sonam to still be downtrodden too, but he looked as if he'd regrown himself in a fresh vat of stem cells. He took a break from his prayers.

"Ah, Ja-ma, many many sleep. Dis good resting."

"How are you, Sonam?" I asked sluggishly. (For months in McLeod, I hadn't touched coffee, but I suddenly needed one like I needed air.)

"Ah, dis morning, I bery happy!"

Oh no, here we go again, I thought. Anything but the happiness train. Couldn't we just wallow? Couldn't we be victims of a cruel universe for the morning?

"Dis visa no problem," Sonam said as if the month of failed work was just a dash of salt he left out of a cake "I tink later, you me Tibet going. Dis time no good."

I rolled over in bed and curled up into the fetal position. I saw that I was clinging to my wallowing and spent about ten minutes criticizing myself for doing that, which heated the wallowing to a nice boil—right where I wanted it.

Part of me wanted to stand up and shout: *Nobody is going home, Sonam! Nobody is reuniting! Do you know how big fucking China is? Tibet is not going to be free!*

But I didn't.

I resolved not to say anything until I'd had caffeine. Sonam and I walked through the hundred-degree morning and had that sweet coffee and milk at a street café the size of a closet, and Sonam managed to make me smile as he played tag with the slum children who were selling malas and packets of chewing gum.

I still felt bad. But my mood improved with the third coffee—downing them like tequila shots seemed appropriate—and during our rickshaw ride to the bus station, when Sonam said, "Ready, Ja-ma, 'Country Roads,' one, two, tree," I faintly, then louder, began to sing into the dust.

Life is old there, older than the trees.
Younger than the mountains, blowing like a breeze.
Country Roads . . .

★ ★ ★

My last week in McLeod, Sati and her friend Kavita arrived to go trekking with Sonam, Tyler (the break-dancing law student), and me. It had been nearly six months since I'd seen Sati, and her almond eyes were still flecked with sparks of jade. Her lemon-wedge smile was still alluring. She was as smart, funny, sarcastic as ever. Still solving all problems of the world. There was chemistry between us, and I kept expecting to fall madly in love again.

But after all this time engaging with the Sati in my head, it struck me now that the Sati I'd been pining after was not this one in front of me. The Sati I'd been trying to love and failing, the Sati I'd been chasing, the Sati who had haunted my dreams, was an idea, a hologram I'd believed could fill the fissures in my heart.

Sati was an exquisite woman. But even with all her compassion and wit, Sati could not glue me back together. We were two ripples on the sea that had drifted together and crossed through each other. Exchanged molecules and skin and ideas. In a way we'd always be together. But the winds had sent us in different directions now. Wholeness was the sea around and inside, pushing forward. Buoying us up.

Inside an ugly motel with red woolen blankets, Sati and I cried and talked about this into the wee hours of the morning. We agreed that we still loved each other. We always would. But we also agreed it was time to be friends, for now anyway, while life was crazy and undecided, which would likely be always.

The next day, Kavita, Sonam, Tyler, Sati, and I hopped a bus to higher mountains. Sonam wanted to wear his sandals on the whole trek, but Tyler convinced him into an old pair of Nikes. None of us had real mountain gear. So, looking like some troop of ill-prepared ravers, we hiked over glaciers and through ancient villages, past hermits' caves, telling jokes, building fires, and eating channa masala from a can.

Sati and Kavita both struck up quick friendships with Sonam. And Kavita asked us on the trail, "Is he *always* this happy?"

"Yes," Tyler and I said in unison.

"Almost spooky, isn't it?" Tyler added.

One evening, we were all sitting around the campfire. Sati and Sonam were comparing Tibetan and Indian curry. Looking at their faces glowing orange in the light of the embers, I thought how grateful I was that Sati had left me. In breaking my heart—as I'd broken hers—she'd forced me up the mountain, a place I may never have come had I not been broken.

If that hadn't happened, I would have never met Sonam, who had widened my narrow path. In his quest to find family while finding himself, he had shown me how to live fully and that it's OK to be human. It's OK to desire and love and strive so long as you accept that you will fail and wilt and crash too. Even if you succeed, you fail. We all fail. We all die. Even the most wealthy, successful, gorgeous people cannot avoid leaving it all behind. But Sonam gave me a certain comfort even with death. Each moment, after all, is a loss, a transition, a change, a dying.

The following week, when I got on another fragile Himalayan bus to Delhi, this time to fly to San Francisco, it seemed both surreal and appropriate that Sonam and Sati were there to say good-bye. I kissed Sati, trying to enjoy it as our last, and embraced Sonam. He gave me a handmade silver ring with the Sanskrit symbol "om" on it.

"Dis ring Sonam make," he said as we both cried happy and sad tears.

To this day, I almost never take the ring off. And I often hear Sonam's voice in my head when I'm in a tough patch: "Ja-ma, you funny. Dis bery sad no problem."

Sonam and I kept in touch for a year after that trip. But then life got busy, and I forgot to write. Sonam's letters tapered off too, and I figured he'd given up on his grand plan to go back to Tibet via the United States. But while working my first real journalism job some years later, I got a call from a New York number I didn't recognize. When I picked up, all I heard was laughter.

"Who is this?" I said.

"Ja-ma," the voice said. "It me. Sonam. I here. I here. Am-er-ica!"

7

To describe a wave analytically, to translate its every moment into words, one would have to invent a new vocabulary
and perhaps also a new grammar and syntax, or else employ a
system of notation like a musical score.

—ITALO CALVINO

When the ocean comes to you as a lover, marry at once.

—RUMI

When I'd seen him speak in McLeod Ganj, the Dalai Lama focused his whole two-week talk on
bodhicitta, a Sanskrit term that is usually described
as the spontaneous resolve to awaken for the benefit of all.

Citta translates roughly as mind, attitude, or
heart. Bodhi translates as enlightened, open, and awake.
And like spring water beneath earth, this awake, positive
attitude—pure resolve—is said to be hiding there in each
of us, even in the most parched, angry, jealous, heart-
wrenching moments. It's often when we finally let our
guard down, in fact, when our hearts crack, that the spring
water of bodhicitta gurgles up.

This is why, the Dalai Lama said, it's important to reflect every day on the world's suffering. Pain can harden us and make us afraid. Or it can make us vulnerable—the doorway to bodhicitta. The difference, the Dalai Lama emphasized, depends on how much we open to the difficult moments as opportunities.

You can hear these things again and again and they often don't mean much. Maybe because I'd been listening through a translator and trying not to gag on the salty butter tea—truly an acquired taste—but they hit me intellectually during the Dalai Lama's lecture. It took meeting Sonam, a friend who was in pain too, to find a strand of bodhicitta in the breakup.

But a good thing about bodhicitta is this: once the spring has broken through, it wants to become a stream, then a river. And coming home from the Himalayas, I wanted nothing more than to go out and *do good*—to wake up and be a genuine grown-up citizen of our democracy. The problem was that I also needed to pay rent. So after freeloading in my cousin's basement in San Francisco as long as possible and loving every minute of surfing Ocean Beach again, I soon took the only paid journalism internship I could find.

The internship was at a legal magazine about free speech suppression. It was also in Washington, DC, about a hundred miles farther from the ocean than I wanted to be. But that was OK. I visited the Lincoln Memorial at the start

of that internship, tracing Abe's marble-etched words—
"With malice toward none, with charity for all"—vowing
to put all those compassion prayers to work. It was time to
save the planet one free speech legal battle at a time!

DC is beautiful. I learned a lot about journalism, the
Constitution, and how to keep your car from being broken into weekly. I learned about networking and power and
how to use vermouth. But I was serving martinis to political
staffers—the night job I had to get because the internship
paid less than minimum wage—then writing by day about
high school kids being censored by their principals. One cold
evening, exhausted and walking near the frozen Potomac, it
dawned on me that I really didn't like this. It also dawned on
me that I was jumping through all these hoops to write for a
living. And I'd set out on this writing path to discover a bit
of what Kafka meant when he said writing "must be the axe
for the frozen sea within us." But after a couple months in
DC, the sea inside me was more arctic all the time. And try
as I might, legal writing was not the axe I needed.

I blamed my problems on location, on bad office chairs,
on computers turning us into disconnected people with
lower back pain. And while it's true this job was not the
perfect fit, the other side of the coin was that I wasn't quite
ready to be so unselfish. The path to enlightenment is defi-
nitely a path of service. But in my experience, if you give
up your selfish desires too quickly you're like the guy rush-
ing to work who puts the scrambled eggs on high while
shaving. You might be OK. But most likely you're going to
end up recooking the eggs with a bloody face.

Without teachers like Sonam around, I was burning the eggs. But as the internship finally ended and I flew back to California, I reminded myself of the Buddha's words: the path "is beautiful in the beginning, beautiful in the middle, and beautiful in the end." Maybe I didn't need to worry about *where* I was if I could just stay grateful to be walking.

So, I formulated a plan with a little more self-compassion. I decided to go surfing.

Before NASA was scouring the galaxy for signs of water, Thales—the pre-Socratic Greek astronomer and mathematician whom many call the first philosopher—left us with this single recorded statement: "Everything is water. Water is all."

The early Japanese didn't surf. But they too believed water was the origin of things. In the *toro nagashi* ceremony— one that is still performed for the dead—paper lanterns are floated downriver to ferry spirits home to their source.

The ancient Polynesians, who started surfing more than three thousand years ago, called the sport *he'e nalu*. *He'e* translates as transforming from solid form to liquid form. *Nalu* refers to the motion of a wave, the slide. Polynesians incorporated this return to liquid into a daily ritual for commoners and royalty. And when the surf was too big even for the kings, it was called *'Awili*, which meant the gods were surfing.

My dad was a surfer—one of the East Coast maniacs

who surfed Jones Beach through the winter in jeans and a wool sweater. He taught us to bodysurf while we were stationed on the US air base in the Azores—volcanic islands with Gulf Stream–heated waters. I still recall squeezing Pa's calloused hands as my sister and I were obliterated again and again in the spume. Shivering with smiles glued to our faces.

When we were relocated to the mainland, Sacramento, I couldn't shake the sea bug. Surf legends—Jeff Clark, Tom Curren, Kelly Slater—were plastered to my bedroom wall. I spent after-school time skateboarding through the suburbs, pretending the concrete had transformed from solid to liquid (he'e nalu).

Suburbia and divorce led me to uncreative teenage rebellion (pyromania, gangster rap, drugs, alcohol). And when I ran away to Maui at sixteen, it was ostensibly to get away from all that. But mostly, if I'm honest, I just wanted to surf. Without quite knowing why, I viewed this Polynesian water-walking rite as my personal toro nagashi—surfboard, a lantern boat. And with each paddle, ride, flop, dive, I was heading home.

The Himalayas had shown me I could be away from the ocean and not pine for it. But DC was not the Himalayas and I needed my saltwater therapy. Sitting meditation was good. Yoga was good. But those static environments were so different from the whir and jolt of modern urban life. Surfing demanded both patience and adaptation, strength and flexibility, all in the ever-changing, ever-dangerous sea. Surfing was zen for the stormy world. And maybe, if I got better at it, I could bring some of that rough-and-tumble zen to the city too. Maybe I could even bring it to a job.

Or maybe this was just a high-minded excuse to go surfing.

Either way, as soon as I sent off my graduate school applications, I fled back to San Francisco, working double time as a barista. The moment I'd saved a thousand bucks, I shipped off to Mexico.

I remember that first Mexican surf. Eastern mountains hid the rising sun. Agave, cacti, and beaucarnea trees seemed to sleep in the still air. Horizon clouds, dark and pearly against a jade Pacific, grew plump with desert rain.

It was sunrise on the Oaxacan coast and I was the first surfer in the water on purpose. I'd never surfed Puerto Escondido, one of the most ruthless of Mexican surf breaks, and I was hoping for solo time before the other surfers paddled out.

Puerto's boorish waves could be dangerous. But with multiple egos—98 percent of them male—flinging sharp fiberglass boards about, the danger could go from predictable to complex.

Today was small for Puerto: wave faces cresting and feathering at about six feet. But halfway through my paddle, I timed a duck dive wrong. A foamy lip pinned me to the sand, and I understood why an Australian friend had emailed a warning: "Small does not equal gentle, mate. Big, and you're at the mercy of the beast."

Fortunately, though, the waves broke against sand rather than the sharp reefs I'd gotten used to during college in Hawaii. And once through the impact zone, I sat up on my board and looked around—Mexican flag flapping in the offshore breeze, water so clear you could see your toenails—and had that sense of being home.

The peace didn't last. In my first two wave attempts, rather than finding that perfect moment to pop from belly to feet then angle along the face of the wave, I stood an instant too late and plunged over—toy boat down a cascade.

I suppose this still felt like a homecoming, just more like coming home and getting punched in the face. I stayed positive.

But as the sun finally peeked over the eastern hills, the telltale silhouettes of other groggy surfers began appearing on shore. And this was not good. If I kept this jellyfish flop up once the macho herd thickened, I'd be given about as much respect as a kid who shows up to a Harley ride with training wheels.

My gut tightened even as I reminded myself that the whole point of learning to find zen out here was to encounter circumstances that mimicked the stress of the human world. I thought of Gary, my angry restaurant manager in DC, screaming at me for breaking a wine bottle. If I couldn't deal with punchy waves surrounded by tropical paradise, doing the thing I loved most, the Garys of the world would always win.

I spent the next few minutes following my breath, reciting positive affirmations as one of my first meditation teachers, Thich Nhat Hanh, had taught me:

> *Breathing in, I am joyful.*
> *Breathing out, I smile.*

In the midst of this, a jade wave—flecked with morning sunbeams—came right to me. And this one had my name on it, even looked the slightest bit friendly. I paddled, the wave lifted me high, I stood, and then—face-planted.

The problem was that I'd never learned to tube ride. And just about every wave coming in at Puerto was a stalwart, slurping tube. Waves like these are the ones you see in surf magazines: crystalline gyres that are so round and arching they look as if you could drive a car through them. They look inviting. They make you want to take a shower under that stream of salt water, and standing inside them looks easy too: allow wave to engulf you, pose, exit looking cool. But what you don't see in those gorgeous photos is that (a) if you stick your head in that beautiful curtain, it will drop you on your face then body slam you, and (b) those peaceful surfers have all had that happen about five thousand times before they looked remotely serene.

Tube riding, I think, should be compared to ballet's fouetté rotation. In a fouetté, the dancer spins repeatedly on the tiptoes of one foot, the other leg making perfectly timed kicks that whip her ever faster. A master dancer will smile at the audience all the while, but this smile hides years of bloody toes.

In Hawaii and California, I'd gotten lucky and happened into a tube or two. But these were cases of the ocean mugging me from behind. I'd been riding along on a gentle, sloping wave when, like a driver who unknowingly rams a sidewalk, the wave hit reef without me noticing. I had no escape. And getting lucky, a sheath of blue fell over me.

"Only a surfer knows the feeling," goes the old Billabong tagline. And it's true. There is something about water swirling 360 degrees around you, a light at the end of the tunnel as your only reference point to solidity, that makes you feel as though you're being birthed by the sea goddess. Sixties surf star Jock Sutherland put the tube-riding experience well: "I do not receive a giant exudence of the senses but rather a totality of their perceptive strivings, or a non-feeling, as it were, of some of the prismatic auras and shimmering spectrums of bright death."

I'm not sure anyone knows what Jock meant. But that's exactly how it should be.

For now, my prismatic shimmering auras were being viewed from the ocean floor while my face was ground into the sand. That first morning was not an anomaly. During week one in Puerto, I went "over the falls" so often, you'd have thought I was trying to invent a new sport: surfer repeatedly flies off board, each time contorting into a strange shape so sunbathers can look up and say, "That had to hurt."

"How come you're not riding the wave part of the wave?" Siri asked me one day after watching me struggle through another bout. Siri was an artist I'd met just weeks before coming to Mexico. We'd fallen harder for each other than either of us had expected, and when I mentioned I wanted to get out of here, Siri said she did too, a reaction that made me like her even more.

Siri was a bit of a drifter as well. Her bohemian parents had fled Madison Avenue in the '60s, driving a refashioned mail truck to San Francisco where they built their own house in Bernal Heights. While I was in India, Siri was traveling through Thailand after finishing art school in Colorado. None of our fly-by-night planning seemed the least bit strange to either of us, which was precisely why we were here in Mexico for two months together without knowing each other that well.

Another thing I liked a lot about Siri was her dry sense of humor. But this remark—why wasn't I riding the wave part of the wave—hit a sensitive spot.

"I'm not going to answer that," I said.

The saving grace, I suppose, was that I wasn't alone. As I watched more surfers paddle out in their fluorescent patterned shorts and three-day-old scruff—all of us looking suspiciously similar given our supposed counterculture roles—I saw plenty of others doing cartwheels down the face. But then one evening, just before sunset, I witnessed something I had never seen. Like a beam of light breaking through the clouds, I saw the tube-riding master I wanted to follow.

The winds had died completely and the sea had taken on an almost oily black surface. With orange and red sunbeams lasering across the dark undulations, the waves looked like molten lava. Prehistoric, full of life.

There were a dozen or so other surfers out, none of them remarkable. But I soon locked in on a local guy waiting far south and outside the pack. Hoping to get out of the crowd myself, I paddled down to him and got a closer look. He was a leathery beast of a human—sleeve tattoos running all the way up to his neck, exactly the profile of human being I hoped not to get in the way of. But as I watched him take off on his next wave, the man's riding was surprisingly gentle, delicate. His board—a single-fin gun made to perform in waves much, much larger than today's—was more buoyant and fast, allowing him to get into the wave a split second earlier than the rest of us. Rather than taking off under the lip, the man seemed to always be on his feet as the wave stood. Most surfers wouldn't have been able to maneuver such a long board on steep waves, but the man was able to pivot into the pocket as though he were part of the system. He chose a high-line to garner speed. Then, intuiting the wave's movement, he dropped to the base and drew out a long, relaxed bottom turn before the crest devoured him. In the tube, rather than bracing in a squat or frantically pumping his legs for more speed, he seemed to have found complete surrender to whatever the sea had in store. He let the ocean lead. And somehow, every single time, she breathed him out.

Watching this man was like watching a hawk swooping for a gopher, a cheetah stalking prey, a corporate lobbyist working a political cocktail party. And it crystallized an idea that had been forming latently: tube riding was enlightenment. I mean, not literally. The sheer number of expert surfers who were also expert assholes was a good reminder of that. But the tube was the perfect metaphor.

Waves arise when air molecules, seeking pockets of low density, blow over water. Like goose bumps, wind forms ripples on the water's skin, and those ripples act as sails, trapping more air. When wind sustains, that energy congeals into hefty mounds of water. Swell.

Energy in motion will stay in motion. So the swells travel, often for thousands of miles, sorting themselves as they move into tribes of similar speed and size, *sets*. From above, these sets appear as a parade of blue objects. Hard. Defined. But this is an illusion. Little water is moving.

The definition of a wave is a "disturbance moving through a medium," and the memory of wind is spiraling through the medium of ocean. Atoms, molecules, cells are bouncing air's message in an endless domino effect—a game of telephone. Each swell is a sort of ghost, an illusion that only looks like a firm set of matter in motion. And people are too. We look firm with our cookie-cutter parameters: head, shoulders, knees, and toes. But the bits of matter that compose our bodies are constantly getting traded out by new water, new food, new air, new chemicals. There is no static amount of stuff that stays with us from birth to death, no lump of clay you could point to and say, "See here I was as a baby, and now I'm stretched to my current size—roughly the same lump I began as."

As the wave only exists as the memory of wind transferring between particles, we are the memory of some primordial, beginningless exhale (the cause that caused the cause of the Big Bang and every Big Bang before it). And we only exist as separate entities insofar as this breath has evolved us to perceive ourselves that way.

So we too are an illusion, a mirage. And the solar system and galaxy and universe around us, all made of tiny subatomic waves, are spiraling wavelike mirages. Realizing this on an experiential level is, they say, what a Buddha sees. It's why a Buddha can enjoy bliss and be unbothered by loss. But usually, we are so caught in the force and swirl of the illusion, we don't have any ability to see through it—to see that it's hollow at its core.

The magic of the tube, however, is that, well, it is already hollow at its core. And there you are, still and poised in the belly of the swirl, unified with it, but also outside its relentless karma. You are one with its force. But unmoved by its force. Seeing the emptiness of everything while enjoying the everything.

Granted, this is a heady metaphor. Maybe a stretch. But seeing the tattooed tube master reminded me how much I wanted to learn how to do what he was doing.

★ ★ ★

The last rays of light disappeared behind a thin layer of horizon fog. And just as the sky was nearly the same color as the water, a dark, smooth swell appeared on the horizon. I paddled hard, ready for my tube—or at the very least a smooth ride to the beach for sunset tacos with Siri.

I felt myself pick up speed and stood a split second earlier, trying to mimic the tattooed tube master. And I sort of did. I stood right in the pocket of the slurping sea, nailed my stance, angled right, and glided down the line.

In front of me, the tunnel began to form, crest throwing outward, hooking with waning sun in its curl. I ducked, ready. Then the sea swallowed.

Again, darkness.

8

Life goes on. No mountain peak impales the sun.
If you come to a break in your path, leap across.

—HAN SHAN

n the days following, the waves got bigger. More unruly. And if I was getting really skilled at anything, it
was removing bits of sand embedded in my scalp. But I
was getting the tiniest bit better at approaching the tube.
Progress was progress. And land life wasn't too shabby.

After realizing we were sharing our beach shack
with bedbugs, Siri had hunted down a Spanish-roofed villa
that overlooked the waves. The place was only three hundred dollars per month, even had its own pool, and we
fell into a good rhythm. We woke up early to meditate,
do yoga, and work on our writing and painting. I'd then
surf the late morning away while Siri took long walks up
the cobblestone streets. Up where hungover gringos didn't
venture, she took photos of straw-hatted farmers drying
chili peppers or women making tamales. Then she came
back to paint them.

Midday was scorching hot. Not even the ocean, which
hovered in the mid-eighties, was refreshing. So we'd lie

under the fans until evening when the offshores returned. Siri then painted or swam in the calm bay to the north, and I'd usually surf again or write. Then we'd meet for dinner.

Life was good. And even if I wasn't surfing like the tattooed tube master, nothing could really get me down with a hammock to lie in and salt-caked eyelashes.

Until it started to. After three weeks of living this schedule, I was noticing something. On an overall well-being scale, this was an upgrade from DC under the fluorescent lights. But it started to strike me too often that things should be better. Which was strange. If you would've asked me as a teenager if I could envision pure happiness, my answer would've gone something like living on a tropical beach in Mexico with a beautiful woman, nothing much to do except surf, be creative, meditate, and eat tacos. But the problem with trying to find contentment in external circumstances, even when the circumstances are great, is that *you* are still there with all those circumstances. And if you ever wonder why billionaires want more, try having just about everything you want and occasionally watch your thoughts—*really observe them*. Pleasure is relative.

Denmark has ranked above any other country in life satisfaction over the last thirty years, and scientists think one reason is their low expectations. "If you're a big guy, you expect to be on the top all the time and you're disappointed when things don't go well," Kaare Christensen, a professor of epidemiology at the University of Southern Denmark told the *New York Times* recently, referring to one of these big happiness studies. "But when you're down at the bottom like us, you hang on, you don't expect much, and once in a while you win, and that's much better."

I was beginning to see the wisdom of this. Every day I spent with this embarrassment of riches, and every day I did slightly better in the surf—meaning, didn't kill myself—I was looking for slightly better riches. Expecting them. Not consciously expecting them. This expectation stuff was more unconscious, a latent prediction that life should always get better and better, bigger and bigger, as if we were all capitalist economies of our own. As if death didn't exist.

There is a word for this in the Buddhist texts that sounds exactly like what it is. *Dukkha.* From Pali and Sanskrit, dukkha is often translated as suffering or stress. The fact that dukkha exists was the Buddha's first teaching—the first Noble Truth. So people often think the first thing the Buddha said was life is suffering. Not exactly true. The Buddha said that life has many pleasures, pleasures he knew well from his life as a prince. It's often said, in fact, that Prince Siddhartha and his wife made such passionate love in the palace, they fell off the roof and hardly noticed. And when he lived with ascetics for six years—fasting, doing yoga, practicing austerities—Siddhartha quickly attained their blissful states. The ascetics wanted Siddhartha to be their successor, but while close to death from living off seeds and roots, Siddhartha took an offering of milk from a village girl and declared that there is actually little benefit in torturing oneself.

The milk offering, as legend has it, made Siddhartha realize *madhyamika*, the middle way. "If the string is too tight, it will break," Siddhartha said. "If it is too loose, it will not play." And when he went to sit under the bodhi tree with this new perspective, eventually seeing the morning star and becoming fully awake, he didn't then harp on what a bummer earth is. He recommended a simple, mindful life. But he also arranged marriages and helped laypeople connect to their ideal jobs. He seemed to appreciate the absolute—the side of reality in which all things are pure and equal—and the relative world with its beauty and sorrow.

So what was the Buddha saying with the first noble truth?

One of my professors in college taught us that dukkha translates literally as having a bad axle hole. The ancient Aryans who brought Sanskrit to India used a lot of horse- and cattle-driven vehicles, and dukkha basically meant an axle that didn't fit well.

So the Buddha's first teaching might be better translated as "Life is a bumpy ride." And he was quite detailed on why, details we used to chant at the monastery: *Jatipi dukkha. Birth is dukkha. Jarapi dukkha. Ageing is dukkha. Maranampi dukkham. And death is dukkha. Sorrow, lamentation, pain, grief, and despair are dukkha; association with the unbeloved is dukkha; separation from the loved is dukkha; not getting what is wanted is dukkha.*

It's true. We are always ageing, always not quite getting what we want, always losing a little of what we love, always associating with people and things that aren't exactly the way we want them to be, and always surrounded by birth and death and sickness. Rather than sugarcoating life, the

Buddha seemed to be saying that all the unpleasant features of life are the wily waves on the surface of the sea. And as anyone who has ever surfed knows, bumps can be jolting and painful. Or they can be the way things are—even fun.

I thought back to DC's fourteen-hour workdays where the bumpy ride was so obvious: *full frontal dukkha*. Here in Mexico, with the exception of getting drilled by the waves daily, I was encountering pleasant things nearly every second. Yet the mind was still caught in constant attraction and aversion: *If I was a little better surfer, writer, boyfriend, I'd be OK. If Siri was just a little less sensitive, a little more into surfing, she'd be perfect. If there weren't quite so many damn tourists here! If I knew I was accepted to grad school, I could relax.*

Siri and I were locked in this type of thinking nearly constantly. Or at least I was. Fortunately, however, if you want to learn, life offers up teachers and mine would soon reveal themselves: a big-wave surfer named Eduardo and two cheerful Italian pharmacists. Oh, and Siri.

I didn't see the tattooed tube master again. He was probably off at some secret break at the end of a long dirt road. Or maybe he was a Mayan sea god who'd just appeared for a few rides.

But there was another surfer named Eduardo whose riding I began to study. Eduardo was not as graceful as the tattooed man. But he was a deft tube rider. He had also just opened a little *palapa* restaurant on the water. Siri and I loved his mango smoothies. So we often ate breakfast there and got to know him.

When I first met him, I thought Eduardo was pretty cool. OK, maybe I wanted to be him. Eduardo looked like a Mexican Mark Wahlberg. He had a girlfriend who modeled in Milan. He owned this hip little smoothie shack, and just about every turn he did could've ended up in *Surfer Magazine*.

Sure, Eduardo had a bit of that too-cool-for-school attitude of people who grow up in tourist towns and never leave. But Eduardo tried to be a nice guy—even gave me a good deal on one of his old boards since my old fish was not quite doing the trick. I was impressed—stoked even.

Siri, however, was wary. And the second or third time we went to the smoothie shack, I started to see that I might not want to be exactly like Eduardo. Eduardo, we soon noticed, talked exclusively of himself, never asking a single question of his customers. And since he had surrounded his palapa with photos of himself surfing, you could kind of see the logic. Second, Eduardo's eyes never settled. They were always darting about. It seemed Eduardo was either worried someone was after him or worried he might miss a hot girl or a great wave. And lastly, when Eduardo talked about his surfing "career"—which was a lot—there was a heaviness.

"I always think I be pro surfer," he told us one morning as he chopped papayas with a machete. "I mean, I surf three hundred and forty days last year! *Three hundred and forty days!* But I guess"—he trailed off—"I don't know—maybe not happen."

The locals all recognized Eduardo as one of the best. Even the silver-mustached man who sold frozen bananas on the beach, donkey in tow, told us: "Eduardo es un superhero! *Todos conocen Eduardo!*" But during competition time, Eduardo often choked.

"Maybe there is something in me that no want to compete, you know," Eduardo said. "But travel and surf as a pro is my dream, like from when I so small."

Maybe because it was what we'd been trained to say, or maybe because we sensed Eduardo's inner fragility, Siri and I encouraged him not to give up his dream. "You're only twenty-five, man!" we said, but when we left the palapa, we started wondering if that was right.

"I don't think I can go back," Siri said as we strolled up the dirt road. "It's depressing. Here he is in this beautiful place, and he's the best surfer, and he's handsome, and he just complains. I always leave depressed."

So, we stopped going to Eduardo's. Instead, we went to another smoothie shop a few blocks away. But I started running into Eduardo in the water a lot. And even when Eduardo was surfing better than everyone, when he botched a ride, he growled or smacked the water. His posture always seemed taut as though he was ready to unravel at any moment but couldn't. I started to feel almost bad for Eduardo, the man with the dream surf life.

"Isn't the whole point to have fun?" Siri asked one evening when we were out to dinner and saw Eduardo getting out from his sunset session. We were eating chile rellenos and drinking Pacifico, tiki torches flickering, a mariachi band singing in the background. The low sun was turning the sky velvet orange, and Siri, up until this question, had been occasionally running down to kick up sea foam and take photos of the birds.

I'd had a rare good day in the waves before dinner, a glimmer of tubular success. And though my mindful half could see Eduardo as a caricature, a lesson in the subtleties of dukkha, the teenage part that still kind of wanted to live Eduardo's life felt defensive.

"Yeah," I said. "It is supposed to be fun. But it's hard to explain if you don't surf."

"Oh, right," Siri said. "It's, like, so beyond words, man."

I chuckled, trying not to be annoyed. But I soon found myself in an unprovoked monologue about Eduardo. And about *the system*.

Like me, Eduardo had come of age in the '80s and '90s, I told Siri. Classic films like *Morning of the Earth*, which portrayed surfers as shamans communing with the gravity of the moon, were long gone. Surfing had now become corporate: soft drink deals, seven-figure endorsements, dads and moms who raised their two-year-olds to be world champs. And surf films, instead of symbols of a life outside the rat race, revolved around how many adrenaline-laced stunts and women in thongs could be packed into an hour. Eduardo had watched hundreds of these videos with his buddies growing up, and they'd been sold an idea of the perfect life: shred hard, go pro, get the girl, get paid to travel to exotic locations, and thou shalt not suffer. But the going-pro part happened only for a few hundred surfers.

Of those, only the top ten were rich and famous. And now women were surfing just as radically as men, but the surf media, on the whole, were still portraying them like Barbie play toys.

So sure, surfing was a way of life, a religion. But that way of life had sold out. Surfing's corporatized cult was colonizing the minds of young surfers the world over, selling them a fairy tale of happiness just so corporations could sell them seventy-dollar surf trunks. Then, rich from their brainwashing, those colonizers—I wasn't quite sure who they were but I knew they were out there—were buying up the coastlines in Africa and South America and Indonesia, imperializing those little fishing towns—towns with beautiful cultures that date back thousands of years—and turning them into a lame reality TV show. Eduardo, I said, was a victim in that system.

I rambled on for a long time about this—feeling a bit above it all and forgetting that I was wearing my own seventy-dollar surf trunks. (I'd gotten them on sale.) By the time I was done, the sun had long since set. Siri looked as if she was out to eat with someone who wasn't really out with her. But she played along.

"Sounds like you might feel the same way," she said. "I mean, you're pretty stressed if you miss a good day of surf. If you have to take the wrong board out."

"We're all pawns," I said sarcastically. But my smile was tense. I suppose some part of me knew that I was ranting about myself, that I'd come to Puerto to find peace amid the ambitious modern world, but that this was also, to some extent, an attempt to never grow up. To keep seeing myself as a victim of the system.

Eager to take the spotlight off of me, I asked Siri if she felt pressure to be part of that elite urban art world that she certainly had the talent to be part of but also seemed aloof from.

"I did in college," she said, "but I just realized I wasn't really enjoying making art anymore so I just stopped worrying about it. If people like my paintings, they like them. If they don't, they don't."

"Just like that?" I said.

"Well," she said, "I guess at first I went through a period of obsessing about it, then hating the snooty art world and its whole black-turtleneck thing. But then I realized I was making myself miserable hating anything. Judging the elite, you sort of become what you hate. I don't know. I guess I realized the art world is like any world, good and bad. It's just what it is. And if you're an artist, you make things."

I'd have agreed if I was listening better. But the moment Siri had started talking, I started wondering whether Eduardo and I really *were* alike.

I realized my bad listening was making me exactly like Eduardo. Then I repeated the words Siri had just said silently so the words actually planted in my brain.

"Exactly," I said. But, like surfing, good conversation is all timing. The response came too late.

Siri looked out at the horizon, quiet, then took a swig of beer as she shot a glance at me. I recognized the glare: the exact one she often gave to Eduardo.

9

*In the deep blue off Diamond Head, running downwind
before the howling trades, kayak all too eager to pitchpole, to
broach. The waves, also wind-inspired, giving chase.*
A following sea.

—THOMAS FARBER

The next morning, I woke to the sounds of thunder rattling our windows. Or I thought it was thunder. As I rolled out of bed, I realized the thunder was the ocean. A long-period swell had filled in overnight, meaning the storm that generated these waves had churned far across the Pacific. Off Japan perhaps. Or New Zealand. I tiptoed onto the patio, trying not to wake Siri, then watched from the balcony, at first wondering where the waves I'd heard were.

They were out there. But the distance of a long-period swell can create fifteen-minute lulls between sets. And when the sets of seven or eight waves finally arrived, they were clear, defined, gorgeous, and green. They also looked like they could roll a Mack truck.

Back knotted up from too much paddling, bruised in every corner from getting pummeled and stomped, I considered walking down the beach a mile to La Punta, a less exposed left-hander where smaller waves crumbled instead of heaved—not much chance for a tube. But then, Siri and I would be leaving Puerto in a week to head back to Oaxaca City. This could be the final day of big swell—the last chance for that memorable tube that would set things right again.

I ran down the cement steps with the board Eduardo had sold me—a six-foot-ten pintail—sprinted over the cold morning sand, and dove into the foam just as the sky was turning from silver to teal. I paddled out between sets and made it without a single duck dive. But even without the waves, you could feel their electricity. Some wild power was out there. My gut twisted at the edges.

Trying to keep those twists from becoming knots, I focused on my breath—*in, out, in, out*—and when a wall of jade did appear on the horizon, fear was there but it didn't take the lead. I paddled steadily. And figuring there were more waves in the set, I paddled over the first. At the crest, I could feel the swell's unusual thickness, and the next wave looked even fatter. But when it leapt at me, menacing and jade, I turned without thinking, took a few strokes and stood. Usually I felt hurried at Puerto. But this wave seemed to pick me up like a grandfatherly giant, almost in slow motion.

I liked to think I was on a super-vertical wave. The reality was that I think this peak went easy on me. But I stayed centered, slid down the face, and rather than my usual high-line, I let myself get the full speed, drawing out a bottom turn on the flats. As the wall rolled right, it began to bend like a bow ready to unleash. This usually signals the wave is going to pitch hard—in other words, tube. But rather than trying to dig in a rail and go for the glory, I let the turn project me forward with its centripetal force. It thrust me easily ahead of the lip. Before I knew it, I was going *too fast*.

Had I slowed myself with a quick turn, I might have gotten the barrel of my life. But enjoying the speed, I just let the wave take me to its end and sped off the back.

I hooted, then paddled back, grinning at this first success. But I've noticed something over the years from all this surfing, talking with surfers, and writing about surfing. Our first wave is often, but not always, our best wave. And this is because we greet it with the fewest assumptions. After that, we are tainted by success or failure and by how identity collapses around each.

Moments later, a green wall, around house-high, appeared on the horizon. It was an outsider, bigger than the set that had just come through. And now I was seeing through the lens of expecting success. A dangerous lens.

I raced for the outside. I dug, heaved, sprinted, and actually made it out far enough to duck barely under the first explosion. But as the next wave warped, ready to plunge, I found myself in an interesting position with three options. I could either

A. try to paddle over the wave, a choice in which I might flip over backward with the lip;

B. leap off my board and swim down—the practical option with little glory; or

C. turn and try a late, potentially heroic takeoff.

The wave sucked me up. And though I could feel myself regretting it, emboldened by the previous ride, I went for option C. I turned and popped, a sort of no-paddle takeoff I'd seen pros do in movies. But as I stood, it quickly became apparent that there was no water beneath me. The wave had sucked its gut in. There was nothing beneath me but air. Lots. I fell for quite some time. And then, like a sledgehammer coming down on a thin nail, the lip drove me, rigid, into my board.

All was muddy, brown, and confused as the sea stirred me into a stew. I didn't seem to be hurt and was glad for that. But I was down long enough to miss breathing. And when I finally surfaced, gasping, I saw Eduardo's board—half of it anyway. The rest was gone.

"Mother—" I shouted, but before I could finish swearing, I had to dive down to avoid the wrath of the next few waves. When that was over, having been spun underwater, defeated psychologically and physically, I flailed in as best I could.

On the beach, I unhooked my leash and looked at the half a board I'd spent much of my money on. When still whole, the board was worth more than I had in my bank account. This thought alone deflated me. But as I proceeded to whine my way up the sand to the dirt road, passing gaggles of surfers waxing up excitedly, I noticed one of them was Angela.

Siri and I had become acquainted with Angela, a mother of two teenage boys, through her inn and restaurant. She was the only woman I'd seen surf Puerto big, and she did it well. Angela didn't look much over twenty-five because surfing, she'd told us, was the fountain of youth. But she also seemed to have a wisdom beyond her years.

Angela saw my board and gave a knowing smile. "We've got some boards you can borrow if you need one," she said. Then she sprinted into the foam.

I watched Angela disappear under a wave, remembering the real accidents that happened here—broken necks and spines and heads. I had no reason to complain. William Blake popped to mind:

> He who binds himself to a joy
> Does the winged life destroy;
> But he who kisses the joy as it flies
> Lives in eternity's sunrise.

I also thought of what Siri had said the night before: aversion to the elite—be it surfing or art or writing or politics—was the same trap as chasing the elite. They were both attempts to identify solely as a tribe—always in juxtaposition to *the other*—rather than seeing ourselves as nuanced individuals who are all part of the human tribe, and crossing between subtribes constantly.

Last night I'd resisted this wisdom. Now that I had been

humbled, it hit me differently. With each success or failure, each joy or pain, I realized that I was always identifying with that fleeting experience rather than, in Blake's words, kissing the experience as it flew. The result was simple. I wasn't flexible like the tattooed tube master. I was more like Eduardo, failing to enjoy the bumpy ride.

10

A good traveler has no fixed plans
and is not intent upon arriving.
A good artist lets his intuition
lead him wherever it wants.

—LAO TZU

hen Siri came back from her morning walks, she was often effusive about the smallest things: a boy she saw carrying helium balloons, an old Mayan woman she spoke to about embroidery. She had that childlike wonder, that rare ability to give every seemingly common color, taste, or texture a second chance at greatness. Her attention to Puerto's less highlighted features always helped me feel as though we were in a small authentic Mexican town rather than the gentrified, surf-colonized center of Mexican drug trade we'd now realized Puerto Escondido was. But the day my board broke, Siri came back with an extra glow.

"I met these Italian guys on the beach!" she announced. "They want to cook dinner for us tonight!"

I'd been in a great mood—feeling a little wise from making peace with my broken board. But dining with Italian men who had somehow made Siri speak in this giddy tone didn't hit me right.

"Why?" I said, more sharply than I'd wanted.

"I don't know," Siri said. "But they're hilarious. You've got to meet them."

"I do?" I said.

If there was one type of food I'd eat forever, it would, without question, be Italian. If I had to live anywhere on earth, I might choose Sicily. Also, I'm usually open to meeting just about anyone on a trip. That's what travel is about. But with the increasing uncertainty around the long-term prospects of our relationship—which I blamed on Siri and she likely blamed on me—Siri and I had both been swinging back and forth between aloof, then jealous, then enamored. It was increasingly rare that our enamored times lined up. At present, I felt that I was the more aloof one. I had a slight wandering eye, swinging back and forth between fantasizing about a family with Siri and about running off to Fiji with that super funny, good-looking surfer girl with a French accent who I knew existed but who hadn't yet paddled into my life.

But with Siri now beaming about hilarious Italian men, the pendulum was flipping.

Jealousy, not surprisingly, is an insecure little creature. Like any bad idea, it needs to surround itself with worse ideas to feel validated. Once you get jealous about something small—a glance, a comment—that little flea wakes and calls all its friends: all the insecurities you've ever felt about your looks or your finances or your intelligence, all those times you felt helpless or ashamed as a kid. All those monsters decide to throw a drunken bonfire and tell scary stories.

"I don't know," I said. "Why don't we just . . . I don't know . . ."

I realized it would be weird for me to turn down our first offer to hang out with other people. Plus, I was now kissing the joys as they flew.

"Oh, come on!" Siri said. "Don't be uptight!"

I walked around the villa looking as if I had something to do, but I kept forgetting what I was trying to look as if I was doing.

Siri had me. She knew calling me uptight would rile my laid-back image of myself. The fact that she knew this about me meant I was far from my desired image of myself.

"OK," I said. "Sounds cool."

That evening, I put on the only collared shirt I'd brought with me, and we walked down the beach to the Italian guys' casita—twice the size of ours. With its own infinity pool.

A tan shirtless man answered the door, and it was worse than I'd thought. He looked like the grown love child of Johnny Depp and Salma Hayek.

"Siri!" he said, kissing her on the cheek as if they were old friends.

"Giancarlo!" she said.

Giancarlo then turned to me.

"*Buona sera*, Jaimal. Siri tell me all about you! Big surfer! Wow!"

"Hi," I said, giving Giancarlo my best bring-it-you-suave-idiot look—a look I hoped came off as ultra laid-back. But also dangerous.

Meanwhile, Piero—equally handsome and wearing an unbuttoned guayabera—was cooking tomato sauce that smelled like it was wafting out of Tuscany. I turned to the window, unbuttoning my shirt a notch, while Giancarlo poured us some wine.

I was wondering what to say. But before I could decide, Giancarlo was pushing steaming plates in front of us.

"*Mangia! Mangia!* Please!"

Fresh crab, mussels, and deep-fried sardines, all garnished with herbs and butter, began appearing, one after the other. The table looked like a spread from *Bon Appétit*'s travel guide down the Italian coast.

"Where did you guys get *this*?" Siri asked, happier, it seemed to me, than she'd been in some time.

"Oh my God, oh my God, I love Mexico," Giancarlo said, topping off our glasses. "Piero and I find all this today in the sea! All of it! I think the Mexico crab want to crawl in your mouth, you know? *Lo mangio!*"

I'm a vegetarian but an undisciplined one. I sometimes make exceptions when special meals are cooked for me. Plus, I didn't want to look like the one rigid guy around the Italian model-chefs. And though the jealous monsters in me wanted to throw all these plates against the wall, my tongue had other plans. The food was on par with the best meals I'd ever had actually in Italy.

But how could I really enjoy myself with these men I was sure were after Siri? Meanwhile, Siri of course was seeming more perfect, more undoubtedly my soul mate, the nicer these Italian men were to her. As he stirred the sauce, Piero said that the wine—a Sangiovese—was one of just two bottles they'd brought from home. The other bottle was not wine at all but olive oil Piero's father had pressed himself.

"*You guys!*" Siri said.

But *come on*. Now they were sharing their *only* Italian wine. I stayed quiet, trying to slump in my chair so as to continue my cool-danger look. But then Piero took me by the arm: "*Ven*, Jaimal. *Ven*."

For a moment, I was positive Piero was trying to distract me while Giancarlo made out with Siri, something Siri would never do, but jealousy can warp the mind into both writing and believing the most outlandish tales. I stiffened up, peering over my shoulder. But Piero was only leading me to the stove. He handed me a spoon.

"Please, please taste," he said. "It is from our *provincia*!"

Often when you're having a good meal with new friends, someone asks, "What was your best meal ever—I mean, *ever*?" I've noticed a lot of people have trouble with this question, which makes sense. By the time you're twenty, you've eaten more than twenty thousand meals. I love this question. To this day—and maybe it was because I had let my expectations drop to watching my girlfriend leave me for two Italian men—I have never, ever tasted anything like

Piero and Giancarlo's pasta. The sauce Piero asked me to taste defies description because it was so mind-bendingly simple. It was in one sense, tomato sauce. According to Piero and Giancarlo, it had only five ingredients. Basil. Garlic. Olive oil. Tomatoes. "And a secret we will never tell."

It was not tomato sauce. And when Giancarlo poured it over handmade fettuccine, which they had made from local flour and eggs, we couldn't stop eating.

I don't much remember what was said after that. But I do remember I no longer worried if Piero and Giancarlo were after Siri. (If they kept this pasta coming, I might have suggested we all live together.) I just recall laughing and laughing and eating and eating. I also remember we found out Piero and Giancarlo were pharmacists from a tiny northern Italian region that spoke a dialect that was unintelligible even to other Italians. I recall them saying, "We eat our way through Mexico for three month! Three month! I love it!" And anything we said that evening, Giancarlo shouted out, "Oh, oh! *Lo mangio!*" I also remember that by the end of the night, I felt as if Piero and Giancarlo were family.

When we left, Giancarlo and Piero kissed us both on the cheeks.

"You have the wine in your blood now," Piero said. "You always welcome our home."

This would've been my cue to feel like an ass. But as we walked back home along the beach that night, barefoot in the warm sea, I was nearly crying with gratitude.

Suzuki Roshi once said, "If your mind is empty, it is always ready for anything, it is open to everything. In the beginner's mind there are many possibilities, but in the expert's mind there are few."

It's hard to have an empty mind. We are experts of noise and scatteredness. But it's not that hard to empty out expectations a little, to pry yourself just slightly more open to life, which was really the lesson of Eduardo, the broken board, and the pasta sauce—one that finally started to sink in just as we were preparing to leave.

Since we'd begun this trip, Siri had been suggesting we go camping at Lagunas de Chacahua, a bird sanctuary the Lonely Planet said we could boat through and end up on a deserted beach. Since the trip involved sacrificing tubes, I'd been dragging my feet on this suggestion. But the next morning, while Siri and I sipped our coffee and attempted to read the news in Spanish, I said, "Why don't we do the bird sanctuary today?"

"Really?" Siri said, skeptically.

"What?" I said. "I like birds. I love birds."

We took one of the rusty provincial buses to the preserve, then hopped a zodiac ride through miles of marshland. The motor made it too loud to speak, but the scenery filled the roaring silence. Storks, herons, pelicans, and spoonbills swooped and dove and waded. It was cooler among the thick trees, and wonderful to be away from Puerto's drunken tourism.

We camped out under mosquito nets that night and the wonderfulness didn't remain. The campsite owner—a squat, ornery woman—insisted on blaring mariachi music until 2:00 a.m., apparently trying to attract a party. The fact that nobody was showing didn't deter her. We slept poorly.

But at first light, we walked a mile down the coast to a neighboring beach where strange, brown stone formations jutted out of the blue sea like petrified dinosaurs. At the end of the beach, surrounded by these rocks, there was a small cove with water as clear as freshly cleaned windows.

The waves here were tiny: barely two feet. No chance of anything but catching a wave and letting it push you gently across the inlet. But I had brought my fat old fish— the only board I had now. And after floating about with Siri, I paddled out and began letting these minuscule waves drift me into the sand.

There was no crowd of surfers here to impress, no competition. And I spent time on the waves like I used to as a boy in the Azores, marveling at how the light passed through the water.

Looking back, nearly every one of those Puerto sessions is a little fuzzy when I conjure it to write. It's as if I watched those waves on a channel with too much static. Expectations too full to register the color. But that evening in the cove, like the first taste of Piero and Giancarlo's pasta, remains clear. I paddled back and forth, back and forth, not caring in the slightest about what the next ride might be like. If any ride came at all.

11

For example, noble sir, without going out into the great ocean, it is impossible to find precious, priceless pearls. Likewise, without going into the ocean of passions, it is impossible to obtain the mind of omniscience.

—THE VIMALAKIRTI SUTRA

When he attained enlightenment under the bodhi tree, the first thing the Buddha said was this: "Wonder of wonders! All beings just as they are whole and complete! All beings are endowed with Buddha-nature! But because of their deluded thinking, they fail to realize it."

This statement was really the first koan. The Buddha went on to teach meditation, ethics, and philosophy for forty-five years. He taught to monks and nuns, kings and criminals. And if all beings are already whole and complete, why did the Buddha go to all that trouble?

Zen practitioners delve into this paradox and conclude that the only difference between a Buddha and an ordinary person is a shift in perspective, a shift from the myopic to the vast, a shift that many masters have explained through oceanic metaphors. Hakuun Yasutani said our Buddha-nature "is like the sea, and each individual is like a wave on the surface of the ocean." To elaborate, spiraling waves (our egos) are caught in their own churn of self-centeredness. We view our borders as firm and absolute, our thoughts and feelings as ours alone, happening only inside the walls of our skin. But that's not even close to true. Our bodies and thoughts are not only interdependent on the world around us; they are just like waves—fluid energy moving through the fluid fabric of reality. This may sound abstract, but all objects exist in relation to other objects. A rubber tire exists because of the rubber tree. A rubber tree exists because of earth, sun, and rain. Earth, sun, and rain exist because of chemical elements. Chemical elements exist because of atoms and subatomic particles. We are all constructed of those tiny particles, and if we could see life at this level, we would see how particles "outside" us constantly move through us, become us, and we move through them, become them too. It's just like watching waves refract and mix at the shoreline. But in meditation, this can be experienced. In looking inward, when the mind truly quiets and can dwell in its primal state, we see and feel that our perception of separation has always been a fractured view. In reality, our individual wave has also always been the same nature as the entire sea. All water.

This shift is visceral but can also be subtle. The wave is still a wave and has to pay taxes. The sea is still the sea. Our interdependence doesn't negate individual responsibility. But when the oceanic *perspective*—the view of an enlightened being—is lived from, the wave is more compassionate to all beings because all beings are part of her body. Though she may still have daily anxieties of workaday life, she has no more deep existential fear or worry for her own future. What is death when water simply turns to water?

This view is often called *oneness* or *nonduality*, but Buddhists more often say nonduality because oneness can conjure a flat ocean where every drop is alike. That misses the point. Every being and thing is unique in infinite ways. No snowflake or ocean bubble is identical, and that must be celebrated while acknowledging that every bubble is the sea and every flake is snow. This is "nondual philosophy" and nonduality itself is simply what we are—*what all things are*—at our very essence: our collective soul of souls.

Nonduality is part of Buddhism, Yoga, and other mystical and philosophical paths too, in which it's often called a name you may recognize: God.

We will get to that. But for now, in Zen, it's worth noting that to experience this state of fluid nonduality, you have to work hard with your meditation practice, be extremely diligent. But you also have to relax and quit trying so hard—a paradox that makes a kind of sense. The experience of the nondual is an actual experience, a destination that infuses one's life with freedom and wisdom. But in each step toward that experience, the nondual is always there inside the very effort being used to experience it. The journey is always the destination. All waves are water, even before those waves break.

This is radical when you think about it. It challenges us not to see liberation or enlightenment as somewhere out there on the horizon, something we might attain some-day somehow if we're lucky and pious. It challenges us to see the muck we're in right now—the stack of dishes, the political fires, the stress, the insecurity—as containing everything we need.

There's an ancient text I often read before bed to remind myself of this. It's called the Vimalakirti Sutra, and it's an homage to a famous student of the Buddha named Licchavi Vimalakirti.

Being a monk is a wonderful thing. But it's not for everyone. And instead of wandering about in a bark-dyed robe, shaving his head, and refusing sex and money, Vimalakirti was a yogi who got involved in politics, social fads, and family life. He even spent time at casinos, the text says, to teach people who weren't usually exposed to spiritual teachings that they too—the profane, the poor, the addicted, the greedy—had an enlightened nature.

I like to think of Vimalakirti as something of a cross between Jeff Bridges's "the Dude," Gandhi, and Leonardo da Vinci. Vimalakirti not only hung out in all the raucous Indian haunts; he also became highly skilled in worldly affairs. "He was honored as the businessman among busi-nessmen," the text says, "because he demonstrated the priority of the Dharma. He was honored as the landlord among landlords because he renounced the aggressiveness of ownership. He was honored as the warrior among warriors because he cultivated endurance, determination, and fortitude. He was honored as the aristocrat among aristocrats because he suppressed pride, vanity, and arrogance."

And the list goes on. Vimalakirti was basically a really kind, talented person. But he balanced his worldly pursuits with the wisdom of nonduality.

The Vimalakirti Sutra first caught my eye when I was leaving Mexico and arriving in New York for graduate school (yes, I finally got in!). Now that I'd found an inkling of equanimity in the wild Mexican waves, it seemed like a good time to give urban life—what my Aussie surfer friends called "the Big Smoke"—another go. It also seemed appropriate to make Vimalakirti my official coach.

I had no illusions that I was bringing enlightenment into the trenches like Vimalakirti. But getting exposed to those trenches made me feel that I was headed in the right direction. New York, bring it on.

From day one of journalism school we were reporters on the beat: police ride-alongs, Robert Moses—esque arguments at city hall, murder scenes in the Bronx, happy hour with our professors. Off the beat, I was losing too much sleep and drinking too many double espressos, losing that balanced California life I'd built an identity around. But that was also part of the plan. "In New York, you can forget, forget how to sit still," Bono sings. And I was so busy now, taking time for zazen and yoga every morning

seemed both quaint and impossible. I let my practice dwin-
dle. And my other sanity regulator, surfing, wasn't easy to
come by on 125th and Riverside.

Not to worry. While interviewing gangsters and crack-
heads, police officers, and struggling artists, I tried to see
that the extreme waves of grad school life were in a sea that
was ever still in the depths. Along these lines, I thought I
could get a little looser on the ethics too. There are many
Buddhist and yogic schools, and they range from conservative to wild. But they all agree that even though our human
ideas of right and wrong may break down in nonduality,
in order to build an enlightened society, we need ethics.
We can't go around lying, killing, stealing, wrecking our
brains with drugs and alcohol, or hurting people with un-
bridled lust.

These are the five precepts. I always tried my best to
adhere to them. But having lived in a Buddhist monastery
where the emphasis on rules could get really intense, where
you couldn't eat a piece of rice after the noon hour without feeling that you should repent for a week, I thought
New York was a good opportunity to chill out. Siri and
I had broken up amicably after Mexico (neither of us was
keen on long distance). I knew I wouldn't be twenty-five
in New York for long. While I was, I didn't want to be an
overrepressed Zen guy who went around judging everyone. I wanted to be cool like Vimalakirti. Kind. But also,
you know, able to show up at the club every now and then.

So occasionally I did. And sometimes that was kind of
lame because shouting at people in the dark while pay-

ing twenty bucks for a drink generally is. But sometimes I ended up with friends at some little dive bar in Brooklyn, dancing like goofballs and feeling alive. A few flings were even had—a tinge of drama.

I was sampling the modern urban way I'd been away from since nearly ending up in jail in high school. Work hard, play hard. And since I was also consuming more news and books than ever before—for once I knew the latest football scores and the names of all the Supreme Court justices—this all felt sort of cool. Intellectual. Even sophisticated.

Sure, I was getting increasingly scattered and exhausted as the semester wore on. But for at least two, maybe three, months I still had a sense this was part of a grand experiment in the wild side of nonduality. Fresh powder covered Central Park in an early season snow, and I remember strolling beneath bare Japanese plum branches, shooting black-and-white photos for my photo documentary course. Watching each flake take its place in the blanket, I imagined myself as a writer in a Kundera novel—life revolving around politics, art museums, and the twists and turns of fleeting romance. And every now and again, seeing the low autumn sun sparkle on the gum-caked, cigarette butt–covered concrete, or watching the Times Square lights radiate over the oily puddles, it really was all light animating this film of New York.

But as fifth-century Ch'an master Hui Neng put it, "concentration is the substance of wisdom, and wisdom is the

function of concentration. Where there is wisdom, concentration is in the wisdom." In other words, lose inward
stability, and you usually start making dumb choices.

As the Hudson froze over, multiple all-nighters writing
about rat infestations in Harlem or the new drug courts
of Brooklyn began spreading my concentration thinner.
And trying to recover with more of the city's relaxation
techniques—movies, music, newspapers, dive bars, sex—
was making me feel genuinely depressed for the first time
in my life. The oneness of it all had flipped from a beautiful
art house comedy to a depressive existential drama.

Two things resulted. I started to get sick a lot: cold, then
fever, then flu. And my decision-making abilities fogged
even more than usual, an experience that culminated in
going out with a group of old friends around Christmas,
one of them an ex-girlfriend whom I had sort of, kind of
been *seeing* at the start of the semester. We had agreed to
just be friends, but it was one of those nebulous things.
Anyway, I arrived at a hip new bar in the meatpacking
district with my ex. She introduced me to her friend, who
was pretty. Drinks and dancing happened. I left with the
friend.

Brain like a jackhammer, still coughing from the stupid,
endless cold, I got an earful the next morning about what
a horrible person I was. I felt like a horrible person too. I
had ignored the most important unspoken precept of all:
Don't be an asshole.

But sometimes you have to feel really awful to change—or at least to remember you can't be flippant about any interaction in this life, big or small. All waves may be water. But all those waves that are people have minds and hearts too. And karma is exactly what they say it is.

My head continued throbbing as we ran newspaper deadline drills in class that afternoon, and all I could think was that I had taken Bono's "New York" song a bit too literally. In the process, I'd torched some central ground rules I'd learned a long time ago. If you don't have an internal peace practice, your stability is linked to external circumstances, which is a terrible peace plan. Also, any time nonduality becomes an excuse for letting go of being a decent human, there's a misunderstanding of nonduality.

I needed help. Vimalakirti lived nearby.

12

The man who had done the leading English translation of the Vimalakirti Sutra, originally in Sanskrit, was a Columbia professor named Robert A. F. Thurman. Thurman was the Dalai Lama's first Western disciple, a man who had lived for years like a Himalayan ascetic before coming back to the United States to get his doctorate at Harvard. He went on to win countless awards and letters, including being one of *Time* magazine's most influential people of the year. He also ran Columbia University's comparative religion program, maintained a nonprofit dedicated to Tibetan human rights, and published dozens of scholarly and popular books. And amid all this, he maintained a rigorous meditation and yoga practice.

But beyond the impressive résumé that is pretty common at schools like Columbia, Thurman was intriguing. With his one glass eye, disheveled silver hair, Tibetan rings on every finger, and wide six-foot-four frame, he looked part Einstein, part retired football coach, part spiritual Mick Jagger. (It also didn't hurt that Uma Thurman was his daughter.) But Thurman's real allure was that he always looked to be having a good time. He had that glint of wily courage in his one good eye. New Yorkers who weren't

even in Thurman's class would fill Columbia's largest auditorium just to hear him weave religion, science, history,
metaphysics, and art like Coltrane improvisation.

I had been accepted to Thurman's dual program in religion and journalism, which meant once I was finished with
this journalism degree, Thurman would be my adviser in
the religion department. And trying to do my second semester a little more wisely, I started auditing one of Thurman's lectures to prepare for the following year.

I didn't have time to go to every class. But the first class
I walked in on was enough to change my thinking. Pacing
across the stage, a crowd of some four hundred students
scribbling notes, Thurman was speaking about the Axial
Age—the time of Buddha and Christ and Socrates—and
its importance in history. As usual, he wove in reflections
from today's news, joking about President Bush and big
cars and our addiction to sixty-four-ounce sodas.

I have no idea what topic his lecture was meant to cover.
But at one point he began describing the Buddhist notion
of the subtle yogic body with its chakras and seventy-two
thousand *nadis*, energetic pathways great yogis can feel just
like their fingers and toes. "In the Axial Age, this was sort
of basic internal science," Thurman said, chuckling. "Now
people think you're on LSD if you even talk about it."

Thurman then made his classic analogy. Outward exploration of the material world, mainly in the West, has
resulted in impressive feats: astronauts can travel through
space; we can split the atom. People often think this is
progress far beyond what less technical societies like Tibet

have produced. But Tibetan masters, Thurman said, simply went the other way.

"The yogis are not astronauts," Thurman said, "but psychonauts—explorers of the mind. They mapped the subtle body and found the internal splitting of the atom—Buddhahood, full enlightenment, which is limitless positive energy."

I liked this analogy. It fit my own theory that spiritual exploration and scientific exploration complement each other and need to work together. But when Thurman began to describe the "extremely subtle body," he called this body "the Buddhist soul." My jaw almost hit the floor. After a decade of hearing various Buddhist masters speak, I had never heard any of them once say the S-word or God to explain Buddhist principles. At least, not since Sonam.

The Buddha said that there is no soul and no creator God. An original creator implies a beginning. And since the Buddha taught cause and effect, how could there be a cause without one before it? A soul implies a fixed, unchanging entity or substance, which the Buddha also refuted because everything relative changes and is interdependent. (Jumping ahead, the Buddha said we each have a "mindstream," an ever-changing energy that reincarnates through beginningless time but is also ever-connected with the substratum of all things.)

"Everything is made in the mind alone," the Buddha also said, which almost sounds as if we individuals are

God. But that's wrong, at least in terms of the individual alone being God. What the Buddha seems to mean by "mind" in this context is not the brain. At the monastery, we chanted the Mandarin word *hsin*, which means both heart and mind. Hsin—as I've had teachers describe it—means both the thinking mind and the mind's fundamental awareness that also connects us to other minds a bit like Jung's collective unconscious. So, when you get down to it, the Buddhist idea of *mind* is similar to what the Hindu traditions, and some mystical Abrahamic traditions, call God. But Sonam was the only traditional Buddhist I knew who made this comparison often; as I listened to Thurman, I remembered a particular metaphor Sonam loved.

I recalled a Himalayan night in May, crisp and moonless. Sonam and I had been mixing the dough for momos, Tibetan dumplings, out on the monastery roof, using a sheet of plywood raised on cinder blocks for a table.

I knelt to help knead the dough, then watched as Sonam rolled out a thin sheet, carved sand dollar–size noodles, and filled each with a pinch of cabbage and cheese. Finally, as if swaddling a newborn, he folded each circular noodle into a careful momo.

"Now you," Sonam said, pushing the bowl to me.

I tried to copy Sonam. But all my attempts ended in piles of dough, cheese, and cabbage that resembled cat vomit.

"Bery good, Ja-ma," Sonam laughed.

I rolled my eyes, determined to better represent American dexterity. But after more failing, I found myself making little dough balls that I hoped would taste like gnocchi. A silence passed until Sonam said, "I tink dis God, Buddha mind bery same same."

"Really?" I said.

It wasn't that this was an uncommon topic for Sonam. When we passed a Catholic chapel in Bhagsunath, he would often say, "I tink dis Christian religion, good religion." But equating God with Buddha mind was new. I asked Sonam for clarification, and he patted a mound of momo dough.

"Dis God," he said.

"OK," I said. "God."

Sonam then chopped God into squares with a butter knife. "These Christians, Hindus, wah wah wah," he said—*wah wah wah* apparently capturing the other few billion theists of the globe. The God that was left over—the stuff between the squares—Sonam gathered up, rolled into a softball-size sphere, and tossed to me.

"Dis love," he said.

"OK," I said.

And I had to hand it to Sonam. If there was one thing I could imagine as all-encompassing love, it was momo dough.

Sonam looked proud as he rolled out a new blob, calling it "Buddha mind," before carving it into small circles too.

"Buddhists," he said.

And again, the dough that had connected the circles, Sonam balled up.

"Com-pash-un," he said, lobbing the ball to me.

I caught the compassion blob and squished it together with the love blob. They were, of course, identical.

"See!" Sonam beamed. "Berrry same same."

I smiled. In theory, I agreed. When I'd lived with Baba Hari Dass, we often used the word *Atman*, the true self or soul, to describe the nature of God, the blissful life force that composes all reality. The Vimalakirti Sutra said "a Buddha-field is a field of pure positive thought," which didn't seem so different from the Judeo-Christian teaching that God is pure love.

But having spent months in India reporting on extremist Hindus and Muslims skewering each other on pitchforks in Gujarat, at the same time that I could see the beautiful momo dough of these faiths, they also made me sick. I asked Sonam why—if fundamental reality was love, and if religion was a doorway to this love—so many religious people seemed so full of hate?

Sonam nodded. "I tink some dumpling no turn out good," he said. "Inside, dis same stuff good dumpling."

He moved my horrid dumplings to the same plate as his pretty ones.

"Dis good religion, good teacher, show all people how find good inside. Dis bad religion say people many many different. Then people many many fight."

I smiled. I had more questions, but part of what made Sonam such a relief to be with was his simplicity. So we moved on to a more pressing topic: how to make Sonam's dipping sauce. We chopped chili peppers and garlic, adding them to vinegar, soy sauce, and honey. But once the dump-lings were cooked, Sonam couldn't help pointing out that the circle dumplings and square dumplings tasted "bery same same."

Sonam then tasted my ugly gnocchi piles.

"Ja-ma," he said. "I tink your momo better next life."

Then, of course, he cracked up.

As I thought back on Sonam, I got a lump in my throat. He seemed to be sitting right in the auditorium, telling me, "Listen dis Professor Thurman. Dis mind many many beautiful."

I listened. That said, I've never been much of a note taker, and Thurman speaks very quickly. So hoping not to misquote him, I've dug up some of his writings that are close to what he taught us.[1] If you imagine Thurman saying this with a few jokes and cackles thrown in, all the while swigging an iced tea, you'll get the point.

"Finally," Thurman said, "there is the extremely subtle body-mind. . . . This is the indestructible drop, called 'the energy-mind indivisible of clear light transparency.' Very hard to describe or understand, and not to be misconstrued as a rigid, fixed identity, this subtlest, most essential state of an individual . . . is a being's deepest state of pure soul where the being is intelligent light, alive and singular, con-

---

1. I'm collapsing time here. These points were actually strewn over a number of lectures and writings by Thurman.

JAIMAL YOGIS

tinuous yet changing, aware of its infinite interconnection with everything. It is beyond all instinct patterns of lust, aggression, or delusion, and makes the boundless process of reincarnation possible."

Thurman said this indestructible drop resided in the heart center. And as I watched Thurman pace, it seemed he was speaking from this place of light aliveness. I felt light and alive too. It was as if Thurman was personally reaching into my chest like that old Tibetan in my dream years before and pulling out this fluid soul. "Behold!"

And yet, at the very same time, the skeptical journalist in me was scribbling down questions. Fortunately, I didn't have to be the class sacrifice.

A man who looked to be in his late fifties and fit the intellectual look well—bow tie, thick round glasses—said that his teacher, a psychologist, taught that Buddha spoke of reincarnation mostly to please Hindus who believed in "that sort of thing." He said the Buddha was actually more of a scientist, that maybe the texts had even been altered after Buddha's death to incorporate Hindu deities and reincarnation.

Thurman grinned. He blew into his hands as if he was stepping up to home plate. "Yes, yes," he muttered, "hmm, hmmm," and began pacing even faster.

Thurman acknowledged that Buddhist texts had indeed changed and evolved. He also massaged the man's ego by adding that this was a good question. These are questions that also came up during the Buddha's life, he said. Even twenty-five hundred years ago there were materialists who

120

believed hard matter was the basis for all consciousness and absolutists who believed only the void—oneness or God— was real, which negated the importance of the individual. But both of these views are extremes the Buddha wanted to break people from.

"The Buddha was never dogmatic about formulae," Thurman said. "He emphasized selflessness when talking with absolutists and he emphasized self when talking with nihilists. But the Buddha always taught a soul as what re-incarnates, as a selfless continuum of relative, changing, causally engaged awareness."

"But," the man interrupted. "Buddhism purports to be a tradition that embraces logic and science, and there is no evidence for such thinking!"

Thurman smiled and rubbed his hands again, then asked the man if he'd ever seen a black hole.

"No," the man replied.

"But you believe they exist?" Thurman asked.

"Yes."

"Why?"

"Because scientists have proven so much that we can observe so I trust that they have also discovered some things that are unseen."

"Precisely!" Thurman said, and he explained how the great yogis ask the same. Students on the path to enlighten-ment should not take anything on faith. When they meet a teacher, they should investigate her logic. They should see if some of the basic, observable teachings are true. Do the teachings on self and mindfulness and ethics relieve suffering directly? Are the other students of the teacher practical and sane? Then, once some trust has been built, a student can begin to trust some of the things that the teacher says about the *unseen* just as we now trust scientists about what they say about the unseen—which, let's not forget, is every bit as wild and mysterious as anything the Tibetans are saying about birth and death.

"Many credible witnesses report that they died and experienced certain adventures," Thurman reminded the class. "Some died clinically and were revived. Some remember as children details and circumstances of former lives, and some of their memories are corroborated by other people, standing up to the investigation of reputable researchers. Some codify the data collected in various ways and present it in manuals in traditions of dying used in many cultures. And the majority of humans in most civilizations feel they must have some concern for the state of their awareness in the future lives they will be obliged to face."

You could hear a pin drop in the room as Thurman rambled on, so many of us no doubt wondering if we believed it. But then, Thurman asked a question that has stuck with me to this day. We think of rational science as liberated and flexible and religion as rigid, but "who is clinging to dogma?" Thurman asked. "What is it that provides materialists the guarantee of a restful nothing awaiting them after death?"

The class was silent.

"No one," Thurman said, "has ever returned to report

entry into nothingness. They have no recorder, no viewer, no extension of their senses into the subjectivity of a dead person. They cannot physically probe into the brain-dead state of any being. They have no convincing description of nothingness, which obviously has no attributes. They have never observed even one material thing become nothing. Why should the energy reality of a state of awareness, be it even a minimal awareness of pure rest, be the exception to the law of physics that energy is conserved and only transformed? What makes the materialists believe so powerfully in the nothingness of that one energy continuum?

"The answer is, obviously, that they have no grounds at all for this belief. It is merely a belief based on brave assertion, corroborated by many other believers, all without a shred of evidence, reinforced by constant repetition and dogmatic insistence. It provides ultimate comfort, satisfying the religious urge to have a complete sense of reality. This comforting nothingness might give rise to suspicion or doubt, so it is disguised for the materialist by the pretense that nothingness is something frightening, something undesirable, a bitter pill that he or she, the brave modern human grown-up, has learned to swallow. This is why materialist scientists are so dogmatically dismissive of evidence about the postdeath continuity of consciousness. They cannot consider the evidence even casually, because this would generate questions about their own belief. Like any religious dogmatism, since it is a logically weak belief, often admittedly irrational, based on no credible evidence, it cannot allow even the slightest questioning, for fear that the resulting doubt could not be withstood."

And then, as if this were just afternoon tea, Thurman looked at his watch. "Ah, look. We've gone over. Have a nice weekend." And he stormed out of the auditorium.

13

loved Thurman's class. It shook me up in just the way I needed shaking. After that one class, I started doing my daily zazen again. Surfing still involved a two-hour train ride and had to be very occasional, but I at least took a few more laps in the pool. I felt better.

As for the life-after-death ideas, I was tempted to say, as I usually did, "Yeah, maybe."

There are lots of types of intelligence. And I'm not sure this means much, but my maternal grandfather, Larry Klar, had a genius IQ. He was even named best mathematician for his class at West Point. Gramp was also a happy man, a dear friend to all his grandchildren, and pushed us constantly to think for ourselves. Gramp said that he was staying agnostic about the soul and God until science could prove it. At one point Gramp even said he might try cryogenics so he could be revived in the future and see if scientists had made any progress on the big questions.

Gramp never did that. He died peacefully in his sleep two weeks after smashing me in a game of tennis. (Also, he did become rather spiritual in his final years.) But I'd decided to take Gramp's approach of rational agnosticism too, which jibed with the Buddha's suggestion to accept nothing blindly but to test out spiritual teachings like a scientist to see if they really did work to relieve suffering. At some point, if you meditate deeply, it's said you will recall past lives naturally. I wasn't there. So agnosticism allowed me to entertain all possibilities without taking anything on faith.

This had worked OK. But maybe because I hadn't been all that great of a spiritual scientist, it also made me feel weak at times—swayed by whatever the dominant view of a culture was. In India, I leaned toward Sonam and his multiple-lives view. At the Ch'an monastery, I could see how perspective changed based on the mind—that belief was relative to other assumptions of culture and geography—and that in any case the body returned to the grass and the sea and the air.

But outside these sanctuaries, surrounded by a culture that seemed clear the afterlife was an opiate of the people, I'd found myself leaning toward that materialist view. This view assumed that consciousness arises from the brain. And when the brain dies, so does consciousness. Anything beyond that was magical thinking.

After Thurman's class, however, it struck me that my agnosticism might be what was also making life in my twenties so unstable. Since turning eighteen, I'd wanted to be a lifeguard one day, a war reporter the next, a scientist one day, a monk the next, a harlot one day, married the next. Part of this was just indecision. But also, if I really looked, these desires fluctuated depending on whether I was running the "screw it, you only live once" view or the "mind and soul are infinite" view.

I was rarely consciously thinking of either of these. We live in a society that worships youth and shoves death under the rug. I wasn't so different. But these two paradigms—one life versus infinity—still swung back and forth in my unconscious, occasionally popping through in dreams and producing different results in life. "You only live once"—YOLO, as the Internet generation puts it—seemed to produce a mix of desperation and existential freedom, a feeling of wanting to get as much pleasure as you could out of this fleeting existence because a long nothing waited without any other consequences or benefits. This was a view that had contributed to some heedless fun but also to stupidity like getting drunk and leaving with my ex's friend that night. The "mind and soul are infinite" view made you want to find internal joy and wisdom so that wisdom would inform where your soul flowed at the crucial transition. Like Pascal's famous wager, this latter view also made you want to pay more attention to that little thing called karma.

Obviously, it wasn't easy to *prove* either of these views was true with a data set.[1]

But maybe if I could get a little closer to settling the pendulum swings between these perspectives, I could get closer to stability—have the right board for surfing the stormiest seas.

I thought about Thurman's suggestion that I should

---

1. There are, however, numerous studies going on at Stony Brook University and other medical schools cataloging that people who clinically die and are resuscitated often have out-of-body experiences in which they see themselves being resuscitated and actually know what was done to them by doctors while they were clinically dead.

look at how my own experiences match up with the yogic teachings, then see if it made sense to trust what yogis were saying about the unseen. So, one spring day after another of Thurman's classes, I skipped a journalism lecture and went to sit under a willow tree in Central Park, the one near the blacktop where the disco roller skaters twirled with their boom boxes and headbands.

Michael Jackson and Prince in the background, my thoughts drifted back to a meditation retreat that had changed my perspective on what is real and unreal more than any other. I'd just finished the yoga-teacher training with Baba Hari Dass and had decided to stay on at his ashram in the mountains above Watsonville (this was a couple years before I met Sonam). Babaji was seventy-seven years old at the time and looked the guru part. He had a long silver beard like Gandalf the wizard. Eyes that could slice you like Ginsu knives—eyes he wielded often because Babaji had taken a vow of silence. For fifty-two years, he had only written to communicate and taught students via chalkboard.

At any rate, toward the end of my semester at the ashram, Babaji was answering questions about the levels of samadhi—those superstates of concentration and bliss that, in both Buddhism and Yoga, are tiered experiences of this nondual awareness. As students asked increasingly frustrated questions about why they'd never gotten to this state, Babaji started giving answers a bit like a football coach tries to fire up the squad ("Anyone can do it with hard work!"). One woman, a new mother, asked him how she could ever find time to dedicate to such meditation in her busy schedule.

Babaji smiled, writing: "You seem to still have time for movies."

The woman looked down.

"Yep. Got it," she said.

I was twenty-one, zealous, and loved this response, loved Babaji's go-hard attitude. And after that lecture I was charged up to go and get samadhi as if it were a mountain I could conquer with enough training. I started meditating three or four hours per day, putting off schoolwork. Then, during break, I took a twenty-dollar Greyhound bus ride to a silent retreat at my old Buddhist monastery, the City of Ten Thousand Buddhas in Ukiah, one of the few places I knew where meditation retreats were still free (no small thing when you're a college student). Sitting beneath a golden statue of Guan Yin, I practiced a secret yoga Babaji had given me when I'd officially taken him on as a teacher. This yoga, Babaji had told me, was meant to be practiced for about two hours per day, and it involved visualizing energy moving through the body's central energy channel, which the ancient texts say runs parallel to the spinal cord and through the chakras. It's also the path the subtle mind energy is said to exit at the time of death.

I knew that I probably should follow directions. But thinking of Babaji's motivational speech, I got a bit carried away. I did the practice all day long. And most of the night.

This felt mischievous because I was breaking Babaji's instructions. But I justified it by thinking, *Weren't all the great sages great rebels?* They all followed the system. Then at some point they bucked it. And crash or succeed, I was going to find my own way, dammit!

I don't think I expected this to actually work, at least not in any tangible way. But about five days into my otherwise ordinary retreat, my spine felt as though it had gone from the usual bony thing that held me up to a Texan superhighway with little vehicles of breath or energy running up and down. I wasn't sure what this meant, but it came with a rumbling from the base of my spine to the tip of my head that felt a lot like sex. I tried not to attach to the pleasure, but I couldn't help liking this a heck of a lot more than having achy knees and praying for the bell to ring so we could go to lunch.

Now, even though I was putting a lot of work into this yoga and meditation stuff, I was never really sure any of this talk of centers in the subtle yogic body, chakras—which mean "wheels" in Sanskrit—was, you know, *real real*. I'd thought I might have sensed them in some rare moments. But I also thought there was a chance that this chakra talk was actually just a way ancient people imagined emotions manifesting in our bodies—a gut feeling, a broken heart, and so forth.

That uncertainty was gone a second later when whatever was happening in my spine caused a tingle in my sternum. The tingle soon became a swirl, the swirl a slow rotation of warmth, and soon, for lack of a better way of describing it, my heart—and not the organ but a distinct wheel-like feature right at my center—felt as though it were getting spun by a contestant on *The Price Is Right*. Faster and faster the heart wheel spun, until the spinning consumed my head and limbs. A flash of heat rushed up me, pinged the crown of my head, and quite suddenly, I felt both like I was having an orgasm in every one of my cells and like I was *gone*. I was just heat, just electricity, just vibration.

I have no idea how long that moment lasted. But when I came out of the state, it was as if I'd done fifteen hours of stretching in the sauna. Usually the meditation schedule at the City was excruciating—hour after hour of still-sitting for fourteen hours. But after that moment, each subsequent hour began whizzing by as if time itself had warped. Not a hint of pain.

Usually if I did a yoga pose, I felt as though I was trying to cram my body into the cookie cutter it was never meant to be in. When I popped into any pose after this heart spin—cobra, triangle, downward dog—I could feel more of what the pose was *doing* inside—directing heat through internal subway tunnels and roundhouse wheels with elaborate branches and petals. Each new passageway in the body seemed to have its own bliss, its own intelligence, and there was a part of me that thought, *Yes, this will last forever. I've made it.*

Unfortunately not.

By day seven, the bliss was fading. I tried hard to hold on, staying up after midnight in the Buddha Hall. But white-knuckling the state backfired. On every retreat I've ever gone on, I have felt pretty good at the end (at least better than I started anyway). But by the end of this one, the sauna bliss had just left me feeling really, really weird. I also had a throbbing headache.

And for *weeks* afterward, I felt off, even a little nuts. Magnetic forces seemed to push at me from left and right. I worried that I'd become one of the classic cases the yogis warn about, a student who doesn't follow instructions and goes insane.

Embarrassed that I hadn't followed Babaji's advice, I didn't even ask him what I should do. Instead, I consulted one of the lay teachers from the Ch'an monastery, Steven Tainer. Steven was more experienced with issues of internal energy than anyone I'd ever met, and he just nodded. "You just did it too much," he said as a parent might to a young child. "Some of these practices are sort of like getting in a rocket ship. You might get to outer space faster. But you also might explode. A steady practice, a compassionate practice, is more important than a high one. You can have high meditation and still be a jerk."

As Steven spoke, I found a renewed gratitude for the simple wisdom of Ch'an—teachings that were all about being here and connecting to nature, not blasting off. I also had a new appreciation for Steven. He wasn't exotic. He didn't wear robes. He didn't look like a guru and actively asked not to be turned into one. He was just an American guy with an ordinary name and ordinary clothes. He also spoke. But he suddenly seemed to be the most enlightened teacher I'd ever met. And since all I wanted after the experience was to feel sort of normal again, to be *home* from this spaced-out feeling, Steven's advice to take it slow and steady—along with tips like keeping the eyes open during meditation and still having conversations during retreats to stay integrated with the world—was exactly what I wanted.

Soon after, I packed up my bags, paid my respects to Babaji, and left the ashram, never to return. And again it was surfing—the pure physicality of it—combined with help from Steven, that eventually made me feel normal again. I still held Babaji in profoundly high regard. But I vowed that my path from that moment forward would be right here on planet earth, toes in the sand. All the metaphysical stuff might be real. But I wasn't going to worry about it yet. I needed to put one foot in front of the other, finish school, get a job, work on being a whole human, and above all, stay sane.

As I looked at the skyscrapers rising up over the oak trees of Central Park, I realized two things. The heart-opening experience had scared me so badly—I really, really didn't want to go crazy—that I'd swept the experience under the rug as I usually swept death under the rug. That denial had helped me get here to New York and into grad school rather than drifting off to who-knows-what ethereal yogic life. (Before that retreat, I'd been contemplating trying to be a monk again.) But it had also kept me from considering the full depth of what Babaji (who also taught about reincarnation) was pointing to, and what Thurman was talking about now.

There are times to dive deep, times to drift on the surface. And maybe I'd had to go shallow for a while to catch my breath.

I felt more free, more integrated, thinking like this. Maybe not as free as the disco roller skaters in the park. Gliding under the leaves in their spandex and aviator sunglasses, they always seemed ahead of the curve in terms of freedom from the oppression of giving a fuck what anyone thinks. But I felt a bit more stable.

There is a limit to memory and conjecture, though. I was still intellectualizing about the unknown, which is like trying to understand a style of music through reading about it.

Regarding the soul, there were always those nagging doubts. Was I just placating my fears?

To believe, I needed to hear the music.

14

I don't want to be the only one here
Telling all the secrets—
Filling up all the bowls at this party,
Taking all the laughs.
I would like you
To start putting things on the table
That can also feed the soul
The way I do.
That way
We can invite
A hell of a lot more
Friends.

—HAFIZ

uring the spring that I was sneaking into Thurman's class, one of my assignments was to make a months-long photo documentary of a person or cultural group—meaning, basically, go stalk some strangers with a camera for a few months, prying into every detail of their lives. This sounded daunting. But hoping to bring the lightness I'd found with Thurman to journalism life, it hit me. Why not profile some Buddhist monks?

Unfortunately the one monastery I found with real monks, on the Upper East Side, charged money just to meditate with them—a fact that made me resent them from the start. Time was growing short. My photography professor was pressuring me to choose a topic already, and I found myself checking out a group of Franciscan brothers who lived in Washington Heights, one of the last rough, low-income sections of Manhattan.

The abbot of the friary—a short man with John Lennon reading glasses—seemed a bit uptight. But I chose the brothers anyway because they were the practical choice. They'd agreed to let me stalk them just about any time. And juxtaposed against housing projects and boarded-up crack houses, guys sporting seventeenth-century robes and beards down to their chests made for pretty good photos.

I'd grown up on the Zeffirelli biopic, *Brother Sun, Sister Moon*, in which Saint Francis gets sick from war. Then, seeing God in nature, he spends his life singing barefoot through the streets of Assisi, healing lepers and rescuing animals. I loved the film. But I'd never spent a minute in a real friary and behind on my deadlines I was now viewing this as a grab-the-good-shots-and-go mission. My expectations were low. Which turned out to be good. As I took the subway to that brick monastery each day to follow the brothers serving food to the homeless or shooting hoops with foster kids, something soon began to happen. I started to like them. A lot.

None of the brothers preached to me, ever. They also

turned out to drink excellent beer, tell good jokes, and laugh like they were in a brothel, though they hadn't had sex in years. In my quest for that quintessential robed-monk baking shot, I'd even run Sonam's momo-dough theory by one of the young brothers, Michael, while he kneaded dough. The big momo sounded "a lot like the way we talk about the body of Christ," Brother Michael said.

Each of the friars had a unique but similar joy about them that reminded me of Sonam. But what I liked most about the friary was swimming.

I took the first plunge one March afternoon. It was snowing lightly on the nearby projects, and I rushed into the chapel, hoping not to miss the brothers' hour of chanting and prayer. As I tiptoed in, I saw the perfect shot—friars, all fifteen or so, lined up like bearded chess pieces beneath the wooden cross. When the abbot peeked up at me, I pointed to my camera.

"This OK?" I whispered. He waved me in.

I quietly snapped shots from different angles. But just as I was standing on one of the pews, getting what I considered a genius aerial view, a tall German friar with a long red beard gave me the universal look for "Seriously, dude?"

"Too loud?" I mouthed. He went back to chanting.

OK. Hint taken. I decided to kneel and wait, which wasn't a big deal. In fact, it was this waiting, this brief pause, that made the difference. The slow Latin chants harmonized in that Gregorian swirl, and within minutes the sounds seemed not just to enter my ears but to penetrate skin and tissue and bone. Like pouring vinegar on baking soda, the sounds both dissolved hard corners of elbow and skull and created a bubbling in the chest. Soon it seemed the friars and I were adrift on an ocean of light and sound.

This may sound melodramatic. But as literature professor Daniel Taylor writes in his romp through the Celtic islands, "If you have . . . ever brushed against the holy—you retain it more in your bones than in your head; and if you haven't, no description of the experience will ever be satisfactory."

I agree with Taylor. But we have all experienced something holy, even if we don't call it that. We are all alive, which is itself holy. Since that's nonspecific, however, I think many of us experience the holy as falling in love or blending into a redwood grove or singing our favorite song at a rock concert.

This brush against the holy at the friary was subtle. Most surprising was how unique and familiar it was. I'd felt this same sensation wandering European cathedrals in high school, chanting in Hindu temples in Indonesia, visiting the hermits with Sonam, or attending silent retreats. When you entered these sanctuaries where human beings gathered to pray and meditate and sing, it didn't matter what the tradition was, what language was being spoken, or even if you understood the rituals and agreed with the philosophy. When you entered one of these sanctuaries, it was as if you had walked into a different inlet of the same ocean. Each cove and entrance had its own distinct qualities, but as you waded into the water, it all had the same thickness, clarity, pressure, salt.

Or at least that was what I felt. The question was

whether I had always been inventing this feeling because I wanted to believe.

I wasn't sure. Perhaps belief and reality are not as far apart as we think. The more I came to the friary, the more I came to sing and pray with the brothers, the more difficult to doubt this aquarium of grace became. I was so inspired, in fact, that I decided to bring the brothers for show-and-tell.

At the time, I was also taking a religion and journalism class, which included a scholarship to report in the Middle East. Ari Goldman, former religion correspondent for the *New York Times*, was our deft professor. "If you want to report on religion," he often told us, "every single piece you write will be ripped apart in more ways than you could ever imagine. That's part of the fun."

Much of what we focused on was how to write a religious scene—the feeling and ritual of faith being one of the most difficult aspects to convey to a reader. So I'd suggested the friars come in to help teach our Christianity unit, giving us a living scene right here in class.

"Sure," Ari had said. "Makes my job easy."

So, duct tape on their sandals, in walked two hooded young friars, Brother John and Brother Julian, to the sixth floor of the journalism school. Brother John looked a little like a younger Paul Giamatti with a thick black beard, while Brother Julian had soft, quiet features: long eyelashes, round green eyes, and a thin blond beard.

I remember feeling slightly nervous for the brothers. Surrounded by chain-link fences, graffiti, drug deals, they'd always looked at home. Here, among all the things they'd given up, they looked a little stiff. Their eyes darted about with expressions that reminded me of the barefoot Saint Francis when, in the *Brother Sun* movie, he first sees the opulence of Rome.

The brothers proceeded to give a fairly ordinary introduction to their mission of serving the poor. They spoke of sacrifice and returning to the simple life. I don't recall much. But I remember that when Margaret, a liberal Italian Catholic, asked if gays could join the brotherhood, John said, "Yes, absolutely," but he used the phrase "homosexual tendencies," reflecting the Vatican view that being gay is something you could choose, even be counseled out of.

Most of us in the class, including me, believed homosexuality was like skin color—not something you could be, or should want to be, counseled out of. Most of us thought it was ridiculous that gays couldn't marry in the Church and, furthermore, that the Catholic Church wasn't in a good place to lecture on sexuality. But as we talked about our differences, the discussion never became angry. The brothers remained serene, humble, and reminded us that they had diverse views. They said Franciscans, like all Catholics, honor the "primacy of conscience." This primacy means that God speaks through our hearts. The

Church makes rules that sometimes change, and these are structural guides. But in the end, we have to follow what we know in our hearts.

"Saint Francis and Jesus," John reminded us, "were revolutionaries."

As the brothers spoke of this primacy, I couldn't help feeling the sea of grace start seeping through the walls of the J-school. I wondered if I was the only odd duck who felt it. But once the brothers said good-bye, Ari nearly leapt out of his seat. "Wow!" he said. "That was like having the monastery come to us! Just their energy alone . . ." He trailed off, perhaps recognizing that *New York Times* journalists don't say things like "their energy."

Ari was a practicing Conservative Jew who once confided he'd been afraid to go near churches as a boy. So the comment seemed to give permission to other students, many secular, to say they'd felt some friar fairy dust.

Jonathan, the gay student, said he disagreed with the brothers on the "homosexual tendencies stuff," but was touched just by their presence. "They're like love toasters," he said. "You just, I don't know, you *feel it*."

Ahmed, an Iraqi Muslim who'd been reporting on the war there, said the brothers made him "see what Christianity is supposed to be."

And later, in the hallway, one of the Jewish single moms pulled me aside.

"I can't stop thinking about those monks," she whispered.

"Yeah, they're pretty great," I said.

"No, I mean, I really can't stop *thinking* about them. Are they all, you know, celibate?"

Granted, this was no scientific poll. But seeing the class's reaction to John and Julian was important for me. I'd assumed my classmates were skeptical journalists who didn't believe in mysticism. Their reaction, however, made me see that both secularists and the faithful can feel mystical presence. We may differ on the fine print, or in how we explain the experience. But maybe, I thought, this basic acknowledgment of grace is part of what makes us human. Maybe I wasn't making this up.

I had this on my mind when our class flew to Israel a few weeks later to report. Ari had scheduled an elaborate tour for us through old Jerusalem, Nazareth, Bethsaida, and Tel Aviv. At each stop, we had interviews with either imams, priests, rabbis, students, soldiers, or gypsies. Like a United Nations panel, these folks had been nicely plucked. They spoke about inclusion and tolerance, two-state solutions and interfaith dialogue, and we the students were starting to feel rather optimistic that faith could still be beautiful, could even prevent war instead of cause it.

At one point, we toured the Jordan River. There was a large African American man baptizing people, and Ari said, "Well, anyone want to get baptized?" A Persian student named Asha said, "Well, when in Rome," and then about six of us followed her, letting the man dunk us in the same river where John the Baptist first dipped Christ.

Again, I felt the grace of the friary in the river—not surprising, I suppose, given my bias toward water. But honestly, it was everywhere in the Holy Land: in mosques and synagogues, on the hillside where Christ multiplied the loaves and fishes, in hummus and hookah shops. The Holy Land felt like a big interfaith rave that never stopped.

Or that's how it seemed for a few days. Soon the headlines caught up.

For example, on our fourth day or so, the class was strolling the stations of the cross, the path Christ is said to have walked as he was flogged in his crown of thorns. It was a sunny day. And we were walking through a narrow limestone alleyway.

I don't remember how we got to talking to the American man with a long white beard, a brown rucksack, and thick bifocals. But he took it as an opportunity to begin preaching that the apocalypse was nigh. Christ would be here to damn the wicked, etc. The speech was pretty boring in its lack of creativity, but the kicker came when he said he would personally destroy the Dome of the Rock— the shimmering Muslim shrine that sat atop the rubble of the old Jewish Temple—with a backpack full of explosives.

"That's the place I'm going to blow sky-high," he said matter-of-factly. Then he marched off, whistling.

★ ★ ★

The second standout moment came at Birzeit University, the largest university in Palestine. I had spent the day on campus, interviewing students for an unofficial poll on extremism. And though I looked high and low, after more than forty interviews, I could not find a single radical. A few female students sheepishly admitted they supported Hamas, but their support, they said, was because Hamas had given them money to go to school. When asked if Israel had the right to exist (Hamas had officially said it does not), they all three said they wanted a two-state solution that included the right of return and the 1967 borders.

The young man I met leaning against the English building, wearing a black leather jacket and jeans, was different. His eyes were bloodshot. He had lost family in the conflict, he said, and that was why he supported Hamas.

"We will not stop," he said, "until every Jew is dead."

The third moment came when I was coming back from Ramallah with a fellow reporter. We were headed through a final Israeli checkpoint to make it back to Jerusalem before dark. There was a long line of Palestinians trying to pass through the checkpoint, and when the soldiers saw that we had American passports, they sent us to the front of the line.

I admit that I was glad for the biased service. The line at the checkpoint had barely been moving, and we didn't have three hours to wait. We had to be back to meet our class. But when a young Russian soldier holding an M16 searched our bags, pulled out my camera, and began scrolling through my photos, I didn't feel so elite.

"What are you doing?" I asked as this woman, who didn't look much over eighteen, eyed the photos I'd spent the last few days meticulously framing. They were photos of the usual stuff you found in Palestine: falafel restaurants, children playing, the inside of a barber shop, military barracks. There were a few shots of bullet-ridden homes or soldiers guarding the new border security wall. But nothing that didn't show up on a daily basis in newspapers around the world. The soldier didn't seem particularly interested in the content of the photos, however, as she navigated to the Delete All button and pushed.

"Hey!" I said, trying to grab my camera back. But it was too late.

"You can't have those," she said stoically as she handed me the camera.

"But you can't just *do* that!" I said, seething.

"God thinks I can," she said.

These examples were cartoonish compared to the horrors that occurred every day somewhere along the borders of the Holy Land. I knew that. But they saddened and angered me more than anything I'd read because for the first time I realized what people in war zones are truly up against. If you had to run into people and situations like this—and much worse—every week, even the most sane, balanced people could turn violent. I was nearly ready to blow something up after my photos were deleted.

After meeting each extremist, I felt myself fall into fear and then into a common trap. The logic, according to this scared and angry part of my brain—and all these emotions seem to come from deep in the amygdala, the lizard brain—went something like this: Religious extremists are violent and insane. Therefore, religion is insane. Therefore, the spiritual experiences that were bringing me so much joy and hope were insane. And therefore, everything was hard, material, random, and cruel. There was no soul, no mind-stream. No enlightenment. No uniting good. No God.

This is a flawed logic. Scientists have invented chemical warfare, DDT, and the atom bomb. Some of them do cruel tests on animals. But this did not mean science is cruel and insane or that the scientific experiments I'd learned from were insane. I'd met journalists who reported on nothing but celebrity gossip and often lied. But this did not mean journalism was shallow and dishonest.

This broad and fearful logic was easy to debunk once it was noticed. But when you are locked in fear, the brain starts to make these associations unconsciously. In Israel, because I was surrounded by wise professors and good friends, I had some insulation from the fear. I told myself I was not going to fall for it. I would, like the friars had recommended, listen to the God of my own heart. Trust my own experiences.

Or I hoped I could anyway. As the trip continued, the characters and situations of hope and faith one minute seemed to be followed by those of fear and hate the next. And for a few days, I found myself on a seesaw between the two.

15

After all this time,
The sun never says to the earth:
"You owe Me."
Look what happens
With a love like that,
It lights the
Whole Sky.

—HAFIZ

tanford anthropology professor T. M. Luhrmann writes that while visiting the Holy Land, "roughly 100 tourists a year become sufficiently overwhelmed by spiritual experiences that they end up in a mental health center. They see themselves as biblical characters or as messiahs, or they feel that they have been given a special task, like moving the Western Wall. Often, but not always, they have had previous psychiatric diagnoses. Some seem to lose touch with reality, and then never do so again. The sheer intensity of being in so holy a place is enough to bring some people to an apparently psychotic state."

Other than finding the best hummus and baba ghanoush

in Jerusalem, I did not think I had a particular calling here. I didn't think I was a biblical character either. And given that I'd met a few crazies already, I was on the lookout for crazy in myself. But many psychologists say falling in love is a temporary state of psychosis too. And it was this state that I could relate to when, at sunset, I came to eat dinner alone on a perch above the Western Wall.

The Western Wall is the last standing wall of Solomon's Temple, the most holy place in the universe for Jews. According to the Hebrew Bible, the First Temple was built in the tenth century BCE and contained, in its most sacred tabernacle, the ark of the covenant, which housed the Ten Commandments God handed down to Moses on Mount Sinai.

The Babylonians are believed to have destroyed the Temple in 586 BCE. But that most sacred tabernacle, the holy of holies, ark and all, is thought to still be buried beneath what is now the Dome of the Rock.

Our other professor—a kind and brilliant man named Rabbi Michael Paley who spoke Aramaic, Hebrew, and Greek—had told us that during Roman and Christian rule of Jerusalem, Jews could only enter the city on a single day every year, Tisha B'Av, to mourn the destruction of both the First and Second Temples. "That's why the Western Wall is sometimes called 'the wailing wall,'" he'd said. But during Jerusalem's Muslim rule (twelfth century to early twentieth), Jews were again allowed to live in the city and worship with relative degrees of freedom, freedom that was expanded when, in December 1917, British forces captured Jerusalem from the Turks, opening the possibility for the current Israeli state.

It was shortly after the capture that British field marshal Edmund Allenby pledged "that every sacred building, monument, holy spot, shrine, traditional site, endowment, pious bequest, or customary place of prayer of whatsoever form of the three religions will be maintained and protected according to the existing customs and beliefs of those to whose faith they are sacred."

As the sinking sun turned gathering thunderheads purple and red, I could see that the sane majority of Israelis and Palestinians had maintained Field Marshal Allenby's goal decently. The Muslim call to prayer—"Alluuuuuuu Akbar"—rang out from the Dome of the Rock while, just below the shimmering gold, a swarm of black-hatted Hasidim and other Jews collected by the wall to daven. Simultaneously, church bells tolled from the area that would have been the Temple's northern wall and was now the Christian quarter.

Meanwhile, I was chowing down on pita and hummus and falafel, none of which I thought I even liked much before coming to the Holy Land. But you have really never had hummus or falafel until you've been to the Middle

East. Comparing the dry, grainy American stuff that tastes a bit like chickpeas and dirt to Middle Eastern hummus is like comparing powdered milk to half-and-half. Anyhow, perhaps it was the dopamine explosion of good food mixed with the sounds of prayer, but I started to feel exceedingly pleasant. I thought of the Dalai Lama's words, "People take different roads seeking fulfillment and happiness. Just because they're not on your road doesn't mean they've gotten lost."

Yes, I thought, and the spiritual bazaar below looked like an interfaith utopia. It also hit me that the scene would be severely diminished—a bit boring even—with just the sights and sounds of a single faith. Why couldn't radicals see that God and humanity were both more glorified by diversity—that diversity *was* the testament to grace?

And then I also thought, *What the hell am I doing?*

Some of my maternal ancestors were Jewish. And even if the only thing Jewish we'd ever done was eat matzo ball soup and light a menorah a few times, as one of the Columbia Chabad rabbis had told me, "You'd be Jewish to Hitler, kid. You're Jewish." Something in me was being called toward that wall.

I gobbled down the final crumbs of pita, licked the plate of hummus clean, then walked down the massive stairwell, blending into the sea of black hats and beards. I suddenly wanted nothing more than to touch the wall.

So, like being at my first rock concert—crowd surfing—I found myself lightly elbowing my way through a thick crowd of the faithful and wedging myself into the front row.

Gigantic limestone bricks, some the size of a small car and looking osseous as woolly mammoth bones, towered before me. In the cracks of those bricks, pilgrims had stuffed pieces of paper that looked like hand-rolled cigarettes: prayers to Adonai, Lord of the Universe.

Looking at the notes protruding from cracks—some on binder paper, others on old envelope scraps, others on handmade parchment—I thought there was something both beautiful and juvenile about this communication method. Could God—the original momo dough of reality—actually care if you wrote the prayers down on paper and stuck them in the cracks of these old bricks versus, say, thinking the prayers—or doing something to achieve those prayers?

I thought not. But then I thought of spinning prayer wheels with Sonam and how nice it had been to see those prayers whirling, tangible. So I took out my reporter's notebook and scribbled down a plea.

"Dear God," it read. "Please, I beg you, wake me up!"

I rolled up my prayer and slipped it into one of the stone cracks. Feeling satisfied, I then decided to push my way out of the prayer pit. I was still hoping to do some reporting on an interfaith Muslim-Jewish soccer team that played in the nearby suburb of Mevaseret Zion, my best chance, I thought, of getting a published clip in the *New York Times*. But when I turned to leave, a group of bearded rabbis holding an immense Torah that looked at least a millennium old had begun swaying behind me, shoulder to shoulder. Some of the men looked not much younger than the Torah they held. And they had sealed me in pretty good. It seemed rude to elbow my way through. So I decided to stay until dark when Shabbat would begin (it was Friday) and the faithful would disperse, heading home for dinner.

I stood at the wall's base feeling a little awkward. But then I decided to quietly chant the name of the bodhisattva of compassion, Guan Yin, one of the few chants I knew by heart.

"*Naaaaammoooo Guan Shr Yin Pu Sa*," I sang softly under the Hebrew din.

Only it felt inappropriate to be reciting Chinese here as an American with Jewish and Catholic ancestors from Lithuania. I quieted down, deciding to just breathe. But in the silence that followed, my right hand on the limestone, the one legitimate line of Hebrew I'd learned from Ari popped into my head: *Baruch atah Adonai Eloheinu Melech haolam*—"Blessed are You, the Lord our God, King of the universe." I started to repeat the phrase, and the sound of the Hebrew had a nice rhythm to it. So I began reciting with more vigor until I was eventually singing, full throated. Almost confident.

The more I sang, the more *Baruch atah Adonai* felt familiar. The recitation was also making me feel a bit more focused, a bit more part of the crowd, a bit more sane.

Then the madness hit.

Hands on the wall and rocking back and forth on my heels and toes like the professional Jews, something struck me that I won't be able to do justice. But in hopes of conveying an epic quality, I will invoke the prophet Jonah to try.

When Jonah was cast overboard by his crew and swallowed into the belly of a whale, he said, "The waters compassed me about, *even* to the soul: the depth closed me round about, the weeds were wrapped about my head. I went down to the bottoms of the mountains; the earth with her bars *was* about me forever."

But just as Jonah felt most trapped by the ribs of the mighty fish, and just before he was spit out, "my soul fainted within me. I remembered the LORD: and my prayer came in unto thee."

I did not think I was Jonah or, I swear, any biblical character. But Jonah's description of remembering God, then being freed from the great whale, matched the way that I felt as my heart seemed to want to leap out from behind my own ribs. I began to cry, nearly delirious in the power that also compassed me about—even, yes, to the soul.

It was a power that collapsed in from all sides. The only appropriate response to this power was to wail as I had not wailed since I was in the Himalayas. Here at the Western Wall, however, I could not run to my private canvas tent and plunge my head in my pillow. The wall of rabbis barred me in like ribs of the whale.

So, even though the tears were ecstatic, I tried to resist. I thought of Jerusalem syndrome. *Let's not go psychotic right in the middle of your first real journalism trip.* After all, perhaps this bawling was simply due to the subliminal messaging of being at the wailing wall. I also thought that I was somehow absorbing, by osmosis, the grief that had been left here through the millennia. I even thought of quantum entanglement, that mysterious principle of particle physics that says when a subatomic particle decays into an entangled pair of particles and those entangled particles separate, whatever subsequently happens to one particle—no matter how distant the two particles become—affects the other particle. They are like twin sisters who eerily know what the other is feeling on the opposite side of the earth.

Was I quantum-entangled with the Jewish people? Was every human? Was that why we all cared so much about this little dot of dirt in the middle of the desert?

But when the bawling became uncontrollable—the sort that feels like you're finally crying for the pain of the whole cosmos—my intellect gave up.

I bawled there for quite some time. Then, as night fell, and the Hebrew died down, I remembered my note written only an hour ago—an hour that seemed like days and nights.

I'd asked God to wake me up. And somehow—seventh-grade note-passing technique and all—God had decided to swallow me up just long enough to peek backstage—back where Rumi's words seemed logical:

*I am neither Christian nor Jew, neither Magian nor
Muslim,*
I am not from east or west, not from land or sea,
*not from the shafts of nature nor from the spheres of the
firmament,*
not of the earth, not of water, not of air, not of fire.

My place is placeless, my trace is traceless.

The sky was deep purple now, and the crowd was thinning. Shabbat was here, the day of rest. Almost as quickly as the rush of tears had begun, they shut off. I looked around and dried my cheeks with my button-down. I didn't quite know what to do. But my feet said walk. So I walked, eventually finding myself back at our hotel, sitting on my balcony, looking out at the night sky.

After a shower and shave, I felt normal enough to speak again. I even ended up catching the tail end of soccer practice in Mevaseret, interviewing the Jewish and Muslim and Christian players about how soccer could save us from war. Then I went to have an evening beer with some classmates.

I slept, woke, ate eggs, toast, and coffee, and prepared for another day of interviews. Work was enough to get me thinking in relative terms again. I never uttered a word about the experience to my friends. (Your credentials as a journalist only go so far once you start spouting off about breaking under the weight of the divine.)

But I could not deny that I was changed. Instead of feeling angry at the American terrorist who wanted to explode the Dome of the Rock, the Israeli soldier who'd deleted my photos, the anti-Semite in Ramallah, I felt empathy, sadness, even love. The innocents these people might harm could always find a way to forgive. But the person who hates is frozen. The hateful are also part of the sea. Nothing escapes. But their hearts are so locked, so cold, so self-obsessed, it's nearly impossible to recall the freedom of love.

Regarding the big questions of the soul, nothing had been *proven* here. But I had to chalk this one up for Sonam and Thurman. Call it mindstream. Call it soul. Call it nonduality. Call it God. I had heard the music in the Holy Land. I believed.

Maybe someday science would prove some soul exists. Maybe not. But unlike Gramp, I realized I didn't need to wait around. After all, if some scientist said she had proven love was *real* right after the first time you'd fallen head over heels, lose-everything-you-thought-you-knew, drunk with the stuff—you know, like, high school prom in love—would it matter to you if you could see the spreadsheet?

16

. . . for I was rich, if not in money, in sunny hours and
summer days, and spent them lavishly.
—HENRY DAVID THOREAU, *WALDEN*

n *Jonathan Strange and Mr. Norrell*, the British fantasy
novel by Susanna Clarke, magic has disappeared completely from England. "Magicians" have become mere
scholars who study the work of the practical wizards of
old like Merlin.

Then, just as the Napoleonic Wars are beginning, a
stodgy, hermetic, cranky old man named Mr. Norrell re-
luctantly decides to reveal that practical magicians haven't
completely disappeared. He gathers the scholar magicians at
an old church and performs the first legitimate spell they've
ever seen. He brings the statues to life.

England will never be the same.

Journalism school ended. I went back to San Francisco for
the summer, and when I returned to New York for my degree in religion, I was thinking of this novel a lot. Clarke
gave language to something I'd long felt about religion in

academia. In almost all my classes to date—though they were each historically fascinating—I felt that we were scholars studying mystical practices that mystics said had to be *experienced* rather than researched. To quote Rumi again,

> *The intellectual is always showing off;*
> *The lover is always getting lost.*
> *The intellectual runs away, afraid of drowning;*
> *the whole business of love is to drown in the sea.*

Scholars seemed to recognize that "drowning" here meant losing our idea of small self or ego, surrendering to God, something all great faiths call for in one way or another. But since you couldn't just go meditating and praying and Sufi dancing for homework, none of us scholars ever approached such experiences in our study. Like the magicians in England, we just talked about how people maybe used to do something like that. Or thought they could.

As this became the way people learned about religion, mystics, it seemed to me, felt increasingly that they had to explain themselves through the language of institutions and logic—the language of the Muggles, as *Harry Potter* fans would put it. Mysticism—practical magic—became increasingly cloistered in secret monasteries while mainstream religious leaders, little by little, became pawns of the Muggles, forgetting their own mystical practices in favor of sounding in sync with the times. The more that happened, the more you wound up with religious leaders teaching laypeople that religion was just about rote memorization, a set of rules, politics. When folks tried to live just a set of rules, they ended up frustrated, judgmental, even angry because there is nothing liberating in identifying with rules alone. They became secret sexual deviants or angry radicals. The magic was gone.

This is of course a generalization. The history of religions is an important subject in and of itself. It should be separated from mysticism. But as I started the master's in religion, I loved classes with Thurman because they felt like a mix of practical magic and scholastic rigor. My other classes, however, didn't. I was beginning to realize that I had no interest in being a scholar. I didn't want to write papers debating who really built the wailing wall. I wanted to understand the grace that had slapped me upside the head at the wailing wall—and to figure out how to get more of that magic in my ordinary life.

There was also money. I'd just come off a summer of magazine writing; a first glimpse at a journalist's salary and city bills. Another practical reality was hitting me. This master's degree in religion was going to leave me with debt that could take decades to get out of. In exchange, I'd have yet another degree in religious studies. I was quite sure not even Thurman had a spell to get me out of that situation.

★ ★ ★

So, hoping I could absorb Thurman's wisdom through his writings and talks and retreats—he would later reveal to me how frustrated he was with academia—I dropped out before tuition time hit and bid New York farewell. Back in San Francisco, I was lucky to find a writing job at *San Francisco Magazine.* The job offered no health benefits. When my reporting hours were broken down, it didn't pay much over minimum wage. But living off burritos in a single-room in-law, I got by.

In that hovel with one window, I shared a kitchen with my landlord, an insurance agent who became strangely enraged if I used a plastic spatula, rather than a steel one, to flip my eggs. But this was worth it. The house was two blocks from Ocean Beach. I could, in addition to working sixty-hour weeks, surf. Also, my editor at *San Francisco* encouraged me to write about what I was passionate about: Warriors basketball, politics, prison reform, my friend's garage band.

I had to occasionally write one of those "Ten Best Secret Beaches!" articles, cringing as I helped make them not secret. I wasn't doing anything terribly mystical. But I also wasn't getting into more debt. I could generally write about quirky characters, social justice issues, and the environment, the last of which I thought maybe could help save our seas from acidifying into a toxic sludge that will turn biological life on earth into a single bottom-feeding species a million years from now. Or maybe not. But I was doing what I had aspired to do on this journalism journey.

★ ★ ★

Absence had made our hearts grow fonder, and Siri and I got back together too. She was living in Berkeley, teaching art at an elementary school, and she and I had a pretty good thing going this time around. We had a fun crew of eclectic friends: writers and surf bums and architects and techies. We went on camping trips to Big Sur, snowboarded in Bear Valley. We watched movies and drank the best wine under sixteen bucks.

Look at us, I often thought. Grown-ups! Working. Buying stuff. Laughing. Crying. Surviving. Even though life was busy, I also felt that I could hold onto a wisp of that grace I'd felt with Thurman and the friars. Each morning while I did my little zazen session, even with my landlord obsessively vacuuming above—why did he need to vacuum *every single morning*?—the Western Wall and the Jordan River and the brothers and Sonam and even the mighty Himalayas were there with me. They were part of my DNA now.

Except, of course, when they weren't. Though I did feel that work and the big momo of reality were becoming more integrated with the mundane, there were still times—lots of them—when I was stuck in my brain spinning about deadlines and whether I'd trapped myself in a career that would never allow me to buy a house in any of the places I loved and whether I would ever feel quite settled in any relationship at all.

But when that sort of frozen thinking happened too many days in a row, Sonam would pop into my head saying, "Dis many many difficult no problem, Ja-ma. Dis make strong." When he had to say that in my ear every day for a month, I knew it was time to go on retreat.

For months, I'd been pretty good about going on little weekend Ch'an retreats with Steven—preempting whatever angst-filled imbalance might set in. But then, the second half of the year, I got a bit overconfident, a bit overly ambitious, and skipped retreats altogether. This led, like an overused dryer filter, to excessive buildup of mental junk, which became apparent one night after I sent in a monotonous piece on the best new gyms in the city. I was feeling frustrated by the pointlessness of such articles, which triggered a feeling that maybe this modern capitalist hamster-wheel life was dumb. I felt that I couldn't keep it up forever and ever. The same uncertainties about my relationship with Siri were also creeping in again. I felt trapped in a cycle of my own mind. And "just as a dewdrop on the tip of a blade of grass quickly vanishes with the rising of the sun," the Buddha said, "the life of human beings is like a dewdrop." And what if my dewdrop evaporated into a blur of deadlines and tasks and imbalanced love so my mind continued into who-knows-what busy, busy next life and so it would go forever? Heedless.

How could the cycle ever end without a radical shift? Without true enlightenment?

I felt freaked out enough that I ended up impulsively spending all my savings on a ticket to a place directly on the other side of the globe that night. And in a few weeks I was on a plane to Bali.

The early Indonesians worshipped the spirits of trees, rivers, and the sea. They were mariners who caulked their boats with tree resin and used that same resin for incense. South Asian merchants began arriving on the archipelago not long after Christ. Local beliefs were absorbed into Buddhism, then Buddhism into Hinduism. "The one substance is called two," a twelfth-century Javanese Buddhist monk wrote, "that is, the Buddha and Shiva. They say they are different but how can they be divided?"

Hindu kingdoms began converting to Islam—largely for trade benefits—around 1500, just about the time the Dutch, Portuguese, and British were competing to control the spice trade in Indonesia. Under all these pressures— colonial, religious—artists and priests from Java and Sumatra escaped to a small island, a lush green dot of lava surrounded by colorful reefs and the warm Indian Ocean, a dot that soon became a refuge of spiritual and artistic freedom.

OK. In truth, Bali has never been just the perfect paradise of peace and creativity and yoga it does a wonderful job selling itself as. Amid artistic resplendency and prayers in the stepped rice fields, there have always been scandals, corrupt governments, wars. As recently as 1965, an ethnic cleansing in Indonesia claimed hundreds of thousands of lives. Many of those murders were perpetrated by the "peaceful" Balinese elite. The island rebounded under a new government, but in doing so, Bali decided to rebrand as an international party destination. Today, areas like Kuta Beach are so thick with massage parlors and pirated DVDs and penis-shaped bottle openers, the Vegas strip starts to seem high class.

But despite government corruption and chintzy wares, it seems to me, after spending nearly a year in Bali over the last decade, that the vast majority of Balinese are a resilient, kind, and creative people. Even when the cops pull you over for a fake traffic violation and demand twenty bucks to avoid a ticket—this is the way they earn back the thousands they have to slip a government official to get the police job in the first place—it's done with a smile. On my first trip, a couple years before the trip I'm now writing about, I forgot my backpack, which contained my passport and laptop, at a bustling market. I came back hours later and found an old lady holding the bag. "I thought you come back," she said smiling. Then she handed me the bag and walked away.

That lady represented the old Bali—apart from elite family feuds, foreign development, and corruption. Made's (pronounced *Mahday's*) was part of that Bali too.

Made's had no telephone, no website, no address, and no computer. You couldn't even drive to the entrance, which was at the end of a long dirt road that didn't have any signs.

But if someone tipped you off or you happened to stumble down it on the way to surf, you were well rewarded.

Made's was a collection of thatch bungalows built illegally on bamboo stilts at the base of a seaside cliff. The huts balanced above coralline coves bordered by volcanic stones so large they looked like a Jurassic species sunning on the shores. At the edge of the sand, a vast reef created pools for wading or swimming, and on the far end of these pools, viridian-hued waves peeled against the shoal.

The price to stay at Made's, if you shared a room, was $2.50 per night. It was five dollars for your own room. But it was best to share because the walls were grass. You were sharing anyway.

A meal of *nasi goreng*—noodles, egg, and vegetables—cost two bucks. A twenty-two-ounce Bintang was one dollar. Coffee was fifty cents. Between surfing sessions, you could lie in a hammock, read books that travelers had left behind, sip fresh papaya juice, and chat with Made and Made, the husband and wife owners of the inn who had the same name because there are only four names in Balinese culture, for both men and women: Wayan, Made, Nyoman, and Ketut. They mean first, second, third, and fourth.

Word about Made's low prices and relaxed vibe had spread to interesting pockets of the globe. When I showed up in July on this spontaneous trip—with little more than my surfboard and a few pairs of trunks—there was a crew of Welsh teenagers who were surfing around the globe before college, a Russian couple who had been doing yoga in India for eight years, two Kiwi surfers living indefinitely off welfare, a Portuguese traveler on holiday from video game production in Shanghai, and Jimmy.

I'd met Jimmy in the water during my first surf trip to Bali. He'd tipped me off to Made's, and we'd struck up a fast friendship. We had a lot of common passions: writing, meditation, surfing, travel. But what I'd come to admire about Jimmy was his ability to thrive at the fringes of the system. Jimmy was pushing fifty but still had no qualms about spending six months of the year sleeping in his van in Ojai, surfing Rincon, and painting houses. He saved up about twenty grand painting each winter. Then, as the Pacific swells faded, Jimmy came to Bali and lived through peak season at Made's.

If all went well, Jimmy could surf through the summer here and still have enough cash to visit friends in Africa, Japan, or Hawaii for a month or two. Then he'd fly home to Ojai and do it all again.

It was an easy lifestyle to spoof. Jimmy himself liked to joke about the Chris Farley *Saturday Night Live* sketch, "You're going to be living in a van down by the river." But Jimmy was happier than any middle-aged person I could think of—a real-life bodhi from *Point Break*. But legal. And not ridiculous. As I thought back to my sixty-hour weeks for thirty-five grand a year with twelve-hundred-dollar rent and five hundred dollars per month in student loans, Jimmy's life looked increasingly alluring.

★ ★ ★

166

I actually didn't see Jimmy for the first week of the trip. Just his boards. Made told me he was traveling on one of the outer islands, merely keeping a room and equipment at Made's until he returned.

"You know Jimmy," the female Made winked at me. "He like a cloud. Come one day, gone next. I don't know."

But one morning when I was just starting to recover from jet lag, I woke to the usual sounds of parrots, macaques, geckos, and Jimmy telling stories down on the lanai.

I peered over the bamboo railing. The Welsh boys, all five towheads, were gathered around Jimmy, leaning in.

Jimmy had better true stories than anyone I'd ever met. He had been imprisoned for weeks for trying to help refugees over the Sino-Tibetan border. He'd been shot in the ass in South Africa. He'd been impaled by a surfing fin in Tahiti. At twenty-five, he was surfing an outer Indonesian atoll and contracted cerebral malaria. Months later, he woke from a coma in a Malaysian hospital, following which he had to learn to talk and walk all over again, a process that took years.

Jimmy looked to be in the midst of another big adventure now. I had to listen.

"There's this stream I go to," Jimmy was saying, holding his bronzed arms to one side to represent the flow of the stream, quivering his fingers like the jitter of rapids.

"It's almost a river, stretching for miles over these curved stones. Some of the stones are perfectly round, and these are the ones you look for. The stones, sort of, I don't know, they call to you—you know. When you're quiet and not really looking. There's that feeling, you know, *that feeling*?"

The Welsh boys nodded.

"Then you look and there one is," Jimmy said, "one of these stones, and it's like, did that stone find me or did I find it?"

Jimmy got into Sisyphean stance, acting out how he rolled these round stones along a riverbed. The end goal was to get the stones to his girlfriend's dad's garden in the Santa Barbara valley, but the journey was clearly the destination.

The stones were huge, he said. So it took hours to roll them back to the house. But then the stone found a groove and rhythm with the current.

"You just roll the stone," he said. "That's all. You don't think of anything else."

"Yeah, mate," one of the Welsh boys said, taking a drag on his Marlboro.

I was wondering how Jimmy had these nineteen-year-olds so gripped by a story about rocks. Not his usual epic. But at the next transition, I understood. This was a way of entering yet another conversation about the subject you couldn't escape for more than a few minutes in this part of Bali: getting tubed.

"Sometimes in the process you come upon a special kind of waterfall," Jimmy said, "where the stream begins to suck up and spill over itself—an aqueous cavern right in the middle of the flow. So you stop. You stop at these little vortices"—he hunkered down on the bamboo floor to demonstrate—"and let that thin sheath of green spill overhead, peering out into the dry world. In there, there's nothing but the echo of water on rock. Time's different. Then you're out again and you just start rolling the stone."

"Siiick," one of the Welsh boys said.

"Yeah, yeah," Jimmy said. "There's something special about tubes. In the river, in the sea, even here"—Jimmy pointed to a far-off lava tube on the peninsula—"in stone."

I wanted to see where Jimmy would take this next. But a fat green gecko began chirping on the roof above me. Jimmy looked up. He smiled his big Owen Wilson smile.

"Jaimal!" he said. "I knew you'd come back."

Because Jimmy rarely emailed or used modern technology like the telephone, he didn't know I'd be showing up. But Jimmy's entire life was a series of surprise encounters. He pointed casually to the surf, which was so feathering and teal and inviting I'd have thought I was dreaming if I hadn't been watching it all week.

"The tide's getting low," he said. "Are we going?"

What I really wanted was breakfast and coffee. But surfing with Jimmy was not to be missed. You learned things just watching him. As social as Jimmy was, I knew that it wouldn't be long before he disappeared again. Sometimes he went and stayed with the locals he called his second family—folks who had nursed him back to health after the coma.

I lumbered down the stairs, guzzled some water and an instant coffee. Ten minutes later, Jimmy and I were tiptoeing across the reef to a break called Impossibles.

When the tide drained on the Bukit, Bali's pinkie-toe peninsula that was absurdly rich with world-class waves, about one hundred meters of reef became exposed to the air. This meant you could no longer paddle to the breaks. You had to walk. At Impossibles, you had to walk over a football field of coral and purple urchins—perhaps the most impossible thing about it.

One wrong step and you risked getting poisonous spines lodged in your foot or slicing a toe to the bone. This could mean a nasty staph infection. Wise surfers wore reef shoes. But I couldn't waste money on those. So I was nearly falling over myself while I tried to keep up.

Jimmy had been walking on reefs so long he strolled on the coral as if on a sandy beach, continuing the conversation we'd floated into about the Indian Himalayas, the place Jimmy was considering returning to this year for meditation.

"Up there," Jimmy said, "it's just sky and stone and white. That's why you need to fill it with infinite flowers, infinite Buddhas, infinite compassion—the wild Vajrayana, you know, and its *dakinis*, its mandalas, its universes inside grains of sand. The mind needs a carrot to chase, a symbol of enlightenment to eventually shatter. It's not like Japan, little islands, precious, precious space, life and green everywhere. Over there, you need zen: white wall, tatami mat. Refine, refine, refine, like sanding a boulder into a pearl. Geography changes a lot."

"Yeah," I nodded, trying not to reveal that my feet felt as if they were being stabbed by tiny spears. Then I looked up.

"Oh fuck," I said.

A thick set began to approach—blue buffalo rearing hooked spines. We were almost to the end of the exposed section of reef and had to decide whether to run to the end and attempt to dive under the breakers, or brace for impact and hope we didn't get grated over the coral.

I looked to Jimmy.

"Well," he smiled. "Off we go!"

He trotted lightly over the coral, making it into the water with enough time to swim under the waves. I tried to follow—"ah, ee, ooo, ouch!"—getting microcuts between nearly every toe. At the last second, I managed to flop into a three-foot-deep area and cling to the coral with my fingertips. The thunderous whitewater skated just overhead. I surfaced, gratefully unscathed, and as I clambered onto my board and paddled toward the horizon, Jimmy was already ten meters ahead in the takeoff zone, turning to catch a long, gorgeous wave.

I watched Jimmy spray peacock tails of water off the back of a blue freight train of Indian Ocean. He was the only surfer I'd ever met who made this break look easy. The waves here peeled fast. If you could tap the power in just the right places to maintain speed, you could ride for a half mile.

Most surfers couldn't carry the momentum. They'd eventually be caught by the foam and sometimes dragged over the reef—the true reason for the name Impossibles. But Jimmy knew exactly the right board to take out—a flat twin-fin fish that skimmed over the surface like a hovercraft—and the right waves to choose. Often, he got several tubes in one wave.

I bobbed quietly, waiting for the right set. Ten minutes later, Jimmy paddled back from his ride with a smile, picking up the conversation as if there hadn't been a break.

"Yeah, India," he said. "I've been feeling it. You ever get that feeling you don't want to go back to the States?"

"Yeah," I said. "Kinda."

This was a strange response because I'd been thinking about it ever since I bought my ticket here. The open road was calling—at least calling part of me. I'd been working the last couple years on repressing this call, for practicality. But now that I'd lived a year of the grown-up life—wasn't that enough already?—Bali had reawakened that urge to jump ship: leave girlfriend, leave magazine, leave student loans, figure it out one day at a time like Jimmy. No health insurance. No retirement. Foam breaking at your heels. Could the IRS find you if you were far enough out? There were seventeen thousand islands in this country alone.

I had also run away enough times that I knew this urge would just be a Band-Aid on the human condition. Wherever you ran to, you still brought yourself—all your whimpering, self-critiquing, complaining. The only escape from those was internal. Plus, another part of me loved Siri, wanted stability, a family, to be part of society, to take care of my parents as they got old, to make some sort of impact with this ridiculously expensive education I'd just purchased. But then I looked at Jimmy and wondered if I was just buying into a societal machine that ground people into depressive drones. Because even if you found noble work and a good work-life balance and a happy family, was it so noble to be just another consumer in a minivan driving your kids to soccer while spewing carbon into the atmosphere? I didn't know. I had a feeling the decision wasn't black-and-white. But my life felt as though it was at one of those *Choose Your Own Adventure* crossroads. The choices seemed to lead to different universes, each with its own booby traps.

"I'm getting the feeling a lot these days," Jimmy said. "I mean, I love to see my friends back in the States and all. I'm grateful for work. But it's not like it used to be there. You think you're going to go back and everything will just pick back up. But then you see people and they're so tired. They're just, I don't know, dead. Just, you know, video games and football and work work work, more more more. Yeah. Dead. They're so stressed about the economy, the economy. Jesus, the economy! OK, yeah, maybe it's bad. But bad relative to what? They don't see what they have. They're not open to just, you know, taking a walk, looking at the sky. You see it in their eyes sometimes. They're just not there—not really."

"Yeah," I said, wondering if I'd been dying a little. If that's why I'd bought the ticket here. But I also wondered if Jimmy had just never grown up—if the coma in his twenties had made him come out like a baby. He still looked like a teenager sometimes with his dancing eyes and goofy grin.

"It's just," Jimmy said, "I don't know. The States have changed. My dad was home every day after school to play baseball with us, take us on hikes. He worked. But he had time. It's the time. It's the time! People don't have that now. But then that's everywhere, right? I guess I'm having a rough go—maybe a midlife crisis."

"You?" I said, a little surprised Jimmy ever had a crisis that didn't involve spring onshore winds. But Jimmy began a long ramble about his girlfriend, Serene. They'd been together five years, and she was wonderful. But she wanted children, a career; she deserved those things. She'd even quit running the old folks' home, a good stable job. She quit to keep coming back here to the Balinese shack, to the Himalayas, to Africa and wherever. She'd done it because she wanted to. Or wanted to at one point years ago.

"But now," Jimmy said with a tinge of sadness, "it's hard to tell. The jig may be up."

Jimmy paused and scooped water in his hands, seeming to contemplate the viscous malleability of it all.

"So I'm thinking the Himalayas," he said, "then maybe go work in Japan. I can chase typhoon swells down there.

I have some old friends there in Tokyo. They have work for me, not like crazy-worker Japanese guys. Surfers, you know, work half-time, surf half-time, drink in the Tokyo alleys at night. Sit zazen with the monks. You'd like it, Jaimal. You should come."

"I've always wanted to go," I said, and Japan did sound appealing. Maybe I could finish the book I'd been working on, get the rest of my tiny advance, then continue on the open road with Jimmy, painting houses, picking up odd jobs. Maybe we'd go back to the Himalayas together. I'd introduce him to Sonam.

But then the student loans and my ageing parents and the career I'd worked so hard to get a toehold in and Siri all started squawking at once on my right shoulder—the one with the halo. Or did I see a pitchfork? How can one know? But I looked at Jimmy's sadness about Serene and where he would live and how he would work. Did I want to be in this same cycle of uncertain relationships and homes thirty years from now?

While I made a Venn diagram of "security" and "freedom" in my head, Jimmy spun from a conversational seated position to grab another long ride. Watching him disappear into blue, I said a silent prayer.

"Give me clarity," I said. "Please."

17

He that wavereth is like a wave of the sea driven with the
wind and tossed.
—JAMES 1:6

And he said all men will be sailors then
Until the sea shall free them.
—LEONARD COHEN

slept hard after the long surf with Jimmy. The next
morning we were out again at Impossibles just after
dawn. The swell had grown overnight. As the sun rose
out of the teal blue, I caught a long racer while waiting
for Jimmy to paddle back from one of his. I couldn't
quite make it as far as Jimmy, but almost. And as my
wave looked to be sectioning out, I kicked off right where
Jimmy happened to be paddling back.

"Yeah, Jaimal," Jimmy said calmly. He had an off-
handed way of tossing out compliments that made them
feel extra sincere. Heaven knows I appreciated the boost.
But Jimmy wasn't looking at me. He was looking west.

"What?" I said, already cringing.

"Not bad over yonder," Jimmy said, nodding toward the peninsula.

Jimmy was suggesting we paddle a few hundred meters away to Padang Padang, a point break often called the jewel of Balinese surfing.

"Oof," I said.

"I know," he said. "Scary. But crowd's not bad. I've been keeping an eye. We could sneak over and grab one or two."

I cringed. The waves at Padang were the things of surf magazine dreams—thick and perfectly hollow. But there were endless stories of surfers getting mangled on the wedge of reef beneath: necks broken, skulls pounded, deaths.

I'd resolved not to surf Padang this trip. I still viewed the tube as a metaphor for enlightenment—the stillness inside the chaos, the union inside duality. But I'd learned my lesson in Mexico. It was counterproductive to push too hard. Before Jimmy had arrived, I'd been getting marginally comfortable at a gentler reef break down the beach called Bingin. That wave, nicknamed "barrel school," was just the right pace for me. But then, if there was anyone who would be good to paddle out to Padang with, it was Jimmy. I hemmed and hawed, agreeing to paddle over with Jimmy and watch.

"Yeah, yeah, just a gander," Jimmy said chuckling.

We began paddling in the channel where we had a perfect side view into Padang's trajectory. Each surge collided into the reef abruptly, flipping and throwing itself outward.

Often the lip of the wave projected wider than the wave's height, and with backlight on the wave's spine, the spiral looked briefly like a teal prism—graceful, gossamer along the fringes. But then the lip connected with the flat sea in a dreadful explosion. The tube formed, and the surfer, if lucky, stayed completely dry in its center before being pushed out by the spit.

"Wow," Jimmy said as we watched a massive wave that nobody dared catch explode. "Swell's building. Almost looks like this wave I used to surf decades ago. Near where I got bitten."

I shot Jimmy a surprised glance. I was pretty sure he was talking about the mosquito that had given him cerebral malaria, something I'd only heard him mention one other time.

"Do you remember anything?" I asked, hoping for a story to help me escape my own nerves. "You know, from all those months unconscious?"

It felt a little taboo to pry into someone's near-death experience. But I'd never encountered a conversation topic Jimmy couldn't roll with and then some.

"Two dreams," he said without hesitation. "In one, I was a Native American and I was tying my wrist together with another man with leather straps, the blood brothers ceremony. In the next, I was in a pyramid-like building, and I was looking down on this horseshoe bay, watching my dad and me walking on the beach when I was a kid. I was in the tip of the pyramid looking through a circular scope, like a long periscope. And then I was lifted up. I saw a conical shape, a being of light, and I was taken into her. I was held by that—whatever it was—and it was bliss. More bliss than I ever believed possible, beyond any idea of what we imagine is possible about happiness or love because, I don't know, it was beyond all that—beyond ideas. I woke up from the coma in the middle of that second dream. I was gripping the nurse's hand. The first words out of my mouth were 'San Sebastián, San Sebastián. I saw an angel. I saw an angel.'"

"Who's San Sebastián?" I asked.

"That's exactly what I wondered," Jimmy said. "You know, my family's religious, but the whole conservative deal in Southern California always weirded me out. I rebelled. But after I recovered from the coma and did all my therapy and that, I went to look him up. Turns out San Sebastián was a soldier in the Roman army. Had to keep his faith secret. When the emperor found out he was a Christian, he had Sebastián shot with dozens of arrows. Everyone thought he was dead—like they thought I was dead—but Irene of Rome, this healer, discovered him and brought him back. Sebastián then went and criticized the emperor in public and he got clubbed to death."

"Geez," I said. "Heavy."

"Yeah. And that's not the weirdest part," Jimmy said. "San Sebastián is also a famous bay in Basque country. I'd never been there when I dreamt of it. But get this—it looks *exactly* like the bay where I saw my dad and me walking in the dream. I've been there now. Yeah. *Really good waves.*"

★ ★ ★

By now, we were drifting into the takeoff zone at Padang. Six other surfers sat waiting, eyes locked on the horizon like some pelagic cult. We both recognized that carrying on a conversation about saints and angels in a pack of adrenaline junkies would be a bit strange. We let the conversation fall away. But all the talk of miracles had me feeling different. I hadn't thought about the wailing wall in many months. Work had consumed me and put me back on the track of judgment and calculation rather than looking at life through a balance of heart and head. Maybe that's why I was feeling so indecisive again—tossed about like an unmoored skiff.

But Jimmy's story had me looking at Padang through something of a wailing-wall lens—a lens of faith. The lens was a little dusty from lack of polish. But it was just enough to recall that there was a piece of me that was not the least bit scared of crashing or not crashing, failure or success, death or life.

This part of me felt just fine surfing or not surfing Padang. But I was here after all—and maybe even for a reason.

I asked Jimmy, "Any words of wisdom?"

Jimmy flashed a grin.

"Believe," he said.

It was bright and sunny, but I felt chilly as we bobbed between sets. I repeated Jimmy's advice silently: *Believe, believe, believe. Believe, believe, believe . . .*

The ocean was calm, and we floated there for a good

ten minutes, waiting for a pulse. When the next set came, it seemed the sea had been storing power. The swells were mountainous as they rose under the sky. My instinct was to paddle for the horizon so none of these behemoths broke on top of me, which was exactly what the other six surfers did. But Jimmy ticked his head toward the beach, urging me to hold ground. Apparently, we were already in the zone.

The first swell began to show boils, tracking the indentations of the reef. The other surfers in the pack began to thrash for it, but they were too far out.

"Go, go!" Jimmy nodded, shouting a whisper.

My brain didn't want to go. But my body seemed to move anyway. Paddling as hard as I ever had, the water sucked me up, up, up to the crest. I stood. But it was too late. The wave was already going concave. And like that, I was airborne.

In that blink of weightlessness, I smashed my back foot down on the board's tail, an attempt to feel the face of the wave, to keep from nose-diving. I knew this was unlikely to stop me. I almost surrendered to a horrid fall. But unlike in Mexico, it worked. My fins touched vertical blue liquid. I landed with my feet positioned on the wax. And I began zooming down the mountain.

The wave was fast and smooth. It shimmered, and I enjoyed the raw speed as I dropped and dropped. But as I transitioned to flat sea, the base of the wave seemed to hiccup. It dropped below surface level, slurping against the reef, and I realized that I had never seen a wave look anything like this. It didn't even look much like a wave. It looked more like a blue-green subway tunnel that had been chopped in half and was falling from space.

The blue circuit warped and bent into a tunnel so long it seemed that I would have to be going the speed of a subway to have any hope of making it to the end. Looking down, I could see the coral seeming to rise toward me. Water can form optical illusions, but there looked to be only a foot or two of water between me and that hard white sharpness.

There was no going back. There is no thinking in these situations anyway. I heard a whistle in my ear as the wind rushed past. I leaned onto my heels, trying to veer left, the direction the wave was peeling. But as the water encased me, it didn't matter which way I wanted to go. The wave was in control now. Just as Jimmy had said, time was different in here. In here, there was just the echo of water on stone. This and this and this. The now—unfiltered. Somehow my board seemed to continue with me continuing to stand on it. Blue, blue, blue. The roar, the roar, the roar. The light at the end of it.

I kept floating through until a burst of foam hit me from behind and I was—could it be possible?—going to . . .

Make it . . .

Out . . .

Please . . .

YES!

No.

In that final meter before the light, a surge of water smacked my head. In an instant, I was flipping cartwheels. Now it was dark. I tucked into a fetal ball, covering my head, praying. Then it happened so fast it was over. My body collided with a hard surface. Like a rubber ball from a vending machine, I bounced back to the surface.

How did a body bounce off coral like that? It seemed impossible. But there I was, gasping and floating in the channel, looking up at Jimmy. He was at the crest of the next wave, making the whole process I'd just been through look dance-like and simple.

Where I had panicked at seeing the wave warp, he leaned forward confidently. He stayed centered, and tucked under the ceiling, dragging his fingers against the blue. His facial expression didn't change as he stood still at the heart of the wave for those few seconds of infinity. Then he blasted out with the spume, hockey-stopping his board just in front of me with calm wild eyes.

"Wow, that was a good one, Jaimal," he said. "Committed."

The wind still knocked out of me, I wheezed and pointed to my back.

"You OK?" he said.

I managed to turn and lift my rash guard.

"Ouch," Jimmy said. "Reef tattoo. But you're moving well. You'll be OK."

My breath slowly returned. I felt lucky. The wave had smashed me directly down onto the reef, rather than along it, and my neoprene rash guard had protected me from any deep cuts.

"Think I'm done for the day," I coughed, trying to smile.

"Yeah, yeah," Jimmy said. "Let's go in."

After what seemed like an hour-long paddle back to Made's, I checked the mirror, and my back looked as if it had been carved up by a sushi chef. But like Jimmy had said, the gashes were superficial. Made even laughed when she saw them. (She'd seen much, much worse living in front of Padang.) Then she helped me clean the wounds with lime and iodine, a process that turned out to be far more painful than the fall.

"Ya, scar good Bali souvenir," Made laughed. "And free!"

Jimmy sat and drank papaya juice with me while the wounds dried, distracting me from the sting with stories about his own reef scars, about kayaking the rivers of Borneo and befriending tribal people.

"You know, I could live out there," he said of a jungle in East Java. "Just plant some mango trees. Eat a little fish, and you're done. You don't really need much, know what I mean?"

"Why don't you write these stories down," I asked Jimmy, knowing he loved to journal. "It would be the best travel book."

"I try, I try," Jimmy said. "I mean, I have journals full, but I don't know, it's like the stories are everywhere. They never seem to find an order. They're sort of out there in the ether. And that's fine. That's where they want to be, I guess. They're for me, you know."

When Jimmy said that, I watched his intelligent blue eyes, and something I'd long sensed about him——but could never put my finger on——became tangible. It wasn't just his stories that were out there in the ether. Part of Jimmy was still out there with San Sebastián. This was why he could drift from place to place, unattached, seeming to skim over the earth.

Jimmy was just who he was. A kind of Ariel sprite, helping lost souls like me. Maybe it was the searing sting of iodine on my back making me not want to follow Jimmy, but I saw that I was not him. I often felt as if I were floating above the world, unmoored. But Padang seemed to be reminding me this wasn't the time to drift.

This time around, for whatever reason, I had to keep close to the sharp earth and human chaos. This wasn't the happy path or the sad path, the perfect path or the imperfect path, the caged path or the free path. It was just my path. I had to look into my heart and trust it because nobody knew it, and nobody could walk it, but me.

I still didn't know where it was going——if I would be a journalist forever, with Siri forever, or living in San Francisco forever. But that night I had a dream that helped me stop grasping at certainty.

In the dream I was dying and a group of doctors were

slowly taking my body apart like a car in a chop shop. First the hair, then the skin, then the eyes. Each time they removed a layer, the world I relied on was melting away. All those memories I stood on like crutches: first kiss, first horror film, first loss, first win. They were each torn away along with the layers of biology. But as the doctors dug deeper, cutting out the intestines, the stomach, the liver, I wasn't afraid. I felt another body beneath this body. It was a body that was woven of mind or wind or water or dreams and couldn't be cut or sliced or killed. I knew this with confidence. Excited about the news, I sat up on the operating table to tell the doctors. But as I did, my excitement woke me. I was sweating—the wounds on my back still stinging.

18

Nature does not hurry, yet everything is accomplished.
—LAO TZU

*I do not understand the mystery of grace—only
that it meets us where we are and does not leave us where it
found us.*
—ANNE LAMOTT

n a famous teaching known as the *sutta* of the arrow,
the Buddha tells his students that, if they hadn't noticed,
even with all this mindfulness and compassion work,
life is still rocky.

"Monks," the Buddha says, "an uninstructed run-
of-the-mill person feels feelings of pleasure, feelings
of pain, feelings of neither-pleasure-nor-pain. A well-
instructed disciple of the noble ones also feels feelings of
pleasure, feelings of pain, feelings of neither-pleasure-
nor-pain. So what difference, what distinction, what dis-
tinguishing factor is there between the well-instructed
disciple of the noble ones and the uninstructed run-of-the-
mill person?"

Buddhist suttas were not originally written down. They

were passed on through recitation. But removing some of the repetition that's there for memorization, the Buddha basically tells the monks that the "run-of-the-mill person," when shot with an arrow, "sorrows, grieves, and laments, beats his breast, becomes distraught. So he feels two pains, physical and mental . . . the pains of two arrows." The person trained in mindfulness, however, when shot with an arrow, feels *only* the physical pain and "does not sorrow, grieve, or lament, does not beat his breast or become distraught. So he feels one pain: physical, but not mental."

With our home team, the Giants, winning three World Series in recent years, this teaching always makes me think of catcher Buster Posey. When Buster gets whacked in the thigh by yet another ninety-five-miles-an-hour slider, he leaps up, cringes, walks it off, then crouches back down for another pitch. It hurts. Of course it hurts. Life hurts. But what Buster doesn't add is a big story on top of the pain. That would just hurt more. There's a game to be played.

After Jimmy flew off to Africa, Siri came to meet me in Bali for the last few weeks of the trip. Before leaving, we had been in the low tide of our relationship cycle, a cycle that usually took a downturn when I started questioning the relationship and Siri got insecure. Then I felt bad, told Siri I was ready to commit, and she proceeded to want out. I then got jealous and tried to convince her to stay. We'd broken up three or four times now, a cycle that was beginning to feel like a depressing *Groundhog Day*.

We were never sure if this breakup cycle was because we both had fears of marriage from our divorced parents or because of something more fundamental. But the fact was this: We had a lot of fun together when we lived in the present. When we thought about the future, the fun got twisted. But instead of letting uncertainty be a single arrow, Siri and I found ourselves complaining about uncertainty a lot, which made uncertainty into lots of arrows.

Maybe it was the Hindu ceremonies where priests in shiny outfits tossed flower petals and holy water on our foreheads. Maybe it was climbing a volcano on Lombok at sunrise or moped rides through mountain rice fields. But in Bali it felt as though Siri and I finally stopped firing arrows at uncertainty. We let uncertainty be its usual uncomfortable self. Then we kept living, two people who happened to like spending time together now.

I presumed this was Bali's magic. But as we immersed ourselves back into San Francisco—working and seeing friends and paying bills and cooking—we were able to keep the good vibes. At least for a while. There was a grace period from uncertainty target practice. And in this period, I also saw that, before Bali, I'd been throwing subtle arrows at the facts of life. I'd been moaning that my student loans took all my money instead of just paying them. I'd been moaning about how much work it took to write a decent article instead of just working hard to write a decent article. I'd been moaning about the onshore winds at Ocean Beach instead of just feeling the wind. I'd been moaning about all the political things that are easy to blame your problems on instead of doing something to ameliorate our flawed democracy.

These arrows had seemed like natural venting, a necessary pressure release. But as I looked at my arrow-shooting habits, I realized that those second arrows never helped. At best, they just were annoying to the people who had to listen. At worst, they made the wounds sting more.

So I tried to completely stop shooting second arrows, and failed. (Complaining is a highly addictive behavior.) But I think I reduced the moaning and whining by about 10 percent. And 10 percent fewer arrows is 10 percent fewer arrows. It can do a lot of good.

For example, now that we'd hit a new stride, Siri and I decided we would try to find an affordable one- or two-bedroom apartment together in the most expensive city on earth, on an art teacher's and a writer's salaries. I was pessimistic about our chances, but I caught myself about to complain and thought, *Wait and see.* Siri, after all, had a way with housing. She had found little lofts or artist's studios by simply knocking on doors of places she loved. This had led to both surprising opportunities and a few frightening experiences. But for Siri, it slanted positive.

So, following Siri's lead, in under a month, we fell in love with a place that was affordable—affordable being a relative term. It was a studio that received perfect morning light and had its own private bathroom and kitchen. That's right, *its own private bathroom and kitchen.*

Siri won the landlord over at the open house, and we were sure we'd get it. But no call ever came, and we eventually badgered the poor landlord enough to discover the truth. A young web engineer had offered two years' rent. In cash.

Similar misses occurred over the next month. Refraining from moaning, I went to the next logical option: quitting. "I think we should throw in the towel," I told Siri one night.

I'd left my little in-law for the Bali trip and was now crashing on my sister's couch. Siri was living in a tiny bedroom in Oakland.

"We can't," Siri said. "This is just the city. You keep trying."

I rolled my eyes. Recently Siri had started approaching strangers on the street to ask for housing. Part of me was impressed. The other part of me thought I was dating an insane person.

"Well, let's do a shelter dance then," I said, trying to stay positive and withholding a second arrow I really wanted to shoot.

"A shelter dance?"

"You know, like a rain dance but for shelter from the rain."

We were taking swing dancing classes at the time—an attempt to find some common passions since Siri didn't surf and I didn't paint. A shelter dance seemed like an opportunity to dance with purpose. Perhaps to pray.

Siri liked this idea. We drew up some pictures of idyllic

apartments. Nothing fancy. Just a couple windows, a roof, a stove, a shower. We taped them to the wall. Then we tossed some ragtime on and began to butterfly, dishrag, and loop-de-loop around my sister's dining room, picturing ourselves settled, happy, cooking.

Sweaty, we then walked down to the beach and burned our sketches in a bonfire. But nothing happened. Nothing but life rolling on, which was OK. Not moaning so much was showing good results in other areas. I'd even landed an opportunity to write a feature about Ocean Beach surfing, something that seemed too good to be true on its own. I never thought the story would tie in to shelter or arrows. But here is how we encountered a single-arrow warrior— the Queen of Ocean Beach—and in the process found an apartment we never could have dreamed up.

There was a new surf shop–art gallery out on San Francisco's foggy western fringe called Mollusk. The Mollusk crew was a cult of scruffy artists who spent most of their days longboarding and drinking boutique coffee on the shop's front stoop. But they also made beautiful retro surf gear and clothing that deified the wave riders of the days past—especially their nonmaterialist ways. Then the crew charged rich folks a lot of money to buy these products.

The Mollusk surfers' obsession with looking as if they didn't care how they looked could feel a little precious. But because many of them had grown up in LA and felt comfortable with the theater of life, they could joke about that hypocrisy, which made them more tolerable than your average hipsters. I pitched the Mollusk crew as a puff piece, and to profile them, I had to interview some of their idols.

"Carol," whispered Jay, a twenty-four-year-old who lived in Mollusk's attic and spent his days building Scandinavian-inspired wooden campers on hatchbacks.

"Who's that?" I asked, wondering why we were whispering.

Jay looked down, shyly twisting his torn wool sweater about his fingers.

"Well, she's actually the Queen."

"The Queen?"

"The Queen."

"Like, literally?"

"Yeah. Of Ocean Beach."

The Queen's palace was just around the corner from Mollusk, a three-story peach Victorian with blue sea horses carved into the beach-facing facade. A life-size Saint Francis mural gleamed on the south-facing wall. Dolphin carvings flanked the third-story dormer window, and a bright wooden sun rose out of the rafters.

I walked up the abalone-embossed steps and knocked.

"Hello? Anyone home?"

Nobody answered, and I was about to leave when I heard a scream. "NO YOU DON'T, YOU LITTLE SHIT!

NO YOU DON'T!" The raspy voice was clearly that of an elderly woman. She sounded panicked, and the front door was ajar. I walked inside.

"Hello?" I shouted, tiptoeing through a living room that was so thick with objects it was hard to find passage. A tarnished tuba lay against a dusty stand-up bass, which lay next to an orange fishing buoy propped on top of a bag of chicken feed.

I climbed over a three-foot pile of yellowing *New York Times* into the kitchen where raw vegetables lay everywhere. Antler-like pieces of driftwood and strands of garlic dangled from the ceiling. I hit my head on one. Then I heard another scream.

"DON'T JUST STAND THERE! GRAB HIM!"

Out of the back window, in the overgrown bougainvillea, I saw the Queen. She was dressed in nothing but batik cloth wrapped around her waist—leathery breasts exposed to the sun, wild red hair encrusted with salt. Her skin was wrinkled and browned like an elephant seal's, but her body was lean and muscular, and she stood like a free safety ready to tackle. Behind her, a fluffy white chicken cowered.

I assumed the Queen was shouting at someone down in the garden, but then she looked directly at me through the window and screamed, "THE DOG! GRAB THE DOG, YOU MORON!" I ran down the squeaky wooden stairs and saw the mutt. He was growling and barking at the chicken as dogs do.

"BACK HOME!" the Queen shouted at the dog. *"Murderer!"*

I grabbed the dog by the collar.

"Where should I take him?" I asked.

"How should I know!" the Queen said.

"OK . . . I guess I'll . . ."

The Queen pointed toward the gate.

"Anywhere but here!" she shouted.

She looked me up and down as if I was dressed strangely.

"Are you looking for somewhere to stay or something?" she asked.

"No, actually, I'm here . . . I mean, I was hoping to interview you."

"Well, does this look like a good time?"

"No, but maybe, you know, another . . ."

"No! I can't do the interview with the dog here. Get her out of here and we can talk. What's your name anyway?"

"Jaimal."

"How do you take your tea?"

That was how I met the Queen, who, I later learned, had lost a few chickens to neighborhood dogs. Over the course of many splendid weeks of interviews with the Queen and her longtime friends, I learned why people left firewood on her doorstep like offerings and how she earned her royal title.

Carol Schuldt was born in San Francisco in 1933. Her step-father was a longshoreman, and her mother stayed home, but "in those days," the Queen told me on that first day in her garden, "parents just said, 'get out of here and be back by dinner.'"

Carol didn't mind this because, "I always had a gang, a big rowdy gang, and we'd go around building caves in the park and having acorn wars, surfing and singing and building fires and getting into trouble."

In her teens, Carol was a wild partier, a terrible student, who ran with some of the beats in North Beach. "Ferlinghetti, the artists and intellectuals, the homosexuals. I was a city girl," the Queen said with a wink. "I played piano at the hungry i all night."

But urban as she was, what Carol truly loved was playing in the cold Pacific. For money, she worked stints on fishing boats and hauled sea logs, but she spent all her free days riding waves with big-wave surfers like Jack O'Neill and Fred Van Dyke who lived around Ocean Beach at the time.

"Your generation doesn't understand, Jaimal," the Queen told me. We were now nibbling raw radishes she'd just yanked up. "You have your gizmos, your technology. You surf and get back in the car. You turn on the heater. You go work in a box not speaking to anyone. You don't stay on the beach. You don't have the fire."

Even after O'Neill, a friend of Carol's, invented the wetsuit in 1952, Carol and her gang bodysurfed Ocean Beach in nothing but trunks or a bikini, a practice the Queen was still maintaining at seventy-five years old (only she usually surfed naked now).

"Life was about feeling then," she said, "not about avoiding pain, not about hiding behind headphones and screens. We were free, Jaimal, and it was wild and not phony at all."

San Francisco seawater hovers around fifty degrees. So Carol's gang gathered driftwood, built a bonfire, then jogged up and down the foggy beach before plunging in.

"We'd stay out until we were blue and then come in by the fire and do it all over again," she said.

"How did you get excited to be cold every day?" I asked.

"It's just cold!" Carol laughed. "What's the matter with that?"

This was back when the palatial indoor Sutro Baths were still standing next to the Cliff House restaurant, when Playland—the beach boardwalk with Laughing Sal and bumper cars—ran along the north end of Ocean Beach where the Safeway is now.

In those days, Timothy Leary was down at the beach keeping the youth stoned. Carol and her friend Tamby, whom she eventually married, led the opposing tribe of healthy surfers, bringing in as many young people as they could. They believed nature was the doorway to truth and managed to buy a small house near the water, often letting friends who couldn't make rent stay with them for free. They also gave shelter to recovering addicts.

"They personally saved me," Rudy Funk, a longtime San Francisco surfer later told me. "They saved I don't know how many people."

But harder drugs were coming to the beach in the late '60s into '70s, and the Sutro Baths burned down in 1966. In 1972, Playland, which was slowly becoming dominated by gangs and heroin, was torn down and replaced with condos.

In Tam and Carol's eyes, these were local reflections of society becoming less in tune with nature each year; the more distant people became, the more drugs and distractions they wanted. Surfers became more aggressive and territorial. A lot of Carol's best friends moved to Hawaii or more rural areas. On top of the cultural shift, Carol and Tam's three-year-old son, Peter, was hit by a car on the Great Highway.

Doctors said that Pete would die or be a vegetable—no hope. But Carol didn't buy it. She ripped Pete off life support at San Francisco General and drove him to Ocean Beach. In tears, she rolled him in the wet sand and cold surf. She believed the sea's power would give him life.

For his first ten years, Pete lived but couldn't walk or talk. Slowly, slowly, however, as Pete was rolled in the tides each morning, and read stories to, and brought to parties, and talked to constantly, he began, for one reason or another, to heal. Broken sentences emerged. Walking, running. By age forty-one, when I met him, Pete's speech was slightly delayed. One eye wandered. His gait was crooked, but he loved to travel and even competed in swimming and running.

Broad-shouldered, blue-eyed, and handsome, Pete often had a girlfriend and did odd jobs around the neighborhood to keep busy. Many called him the neighborhood Buddha for his peaceful, warm demeanor.

Carol and Tam later divorced, Tam moving to a quiet area of Marin. Carol stopped surfing Ocean Beach and began riding her rusted beach cruiser to a beach she called "the pretty place," a secret spot she made me swear not to mention because "it's the last one, Jaimal, the last place where I can connect to the universal mind."

"The ecstasy was over," Tam later told me from his forest cabin, "but through all the madness, what amazes me is that Carol stuck to her values and her lifestyle. She's been through so much, but she never gave up on her ways or wanting to help people, even the people who simply can't be helped. That's why she's the Queen."

I included the Queen in the larger piece about Mollusk and Ocean Beach. Then I moved on to writing about some city controversy or the best fish tacos. But the Queen's voice stuck with me. When I was tempted to moan, along with Sonam, I now heard Carol cackling, "Jaimal, it's just cold! What's the matter with that?"

Inspirational though she was, I didn't think I'd be one of the Queen's many rescues. I'd gotten my drug experimenting done in high school. I wasn't an alcoholic. I even had a job.

One day in spring, however, Siri and I were having lunch on Ocean Beach, not far from where we'd burned our apartment sketches. Afterward, I went surfing, and Siri went walking.

It was a crisp day, offshore winds keeping the sea alert. I was feeling renewed after my paddle. But when I saw Siri from afar, it looked as if she had stumbled on the grail. She was dancing on the beach in little spins. When she came closer, her green eyes were bubbling.

"Wait till you hear this!" Siri said, galloping toward me.

"I'm ready."

"Remember the Queen of Ocean Beach?"

"I think about her every time I put on my wetsuit," I said.

"Well, I ran into her on the beach and introduced myself."

"Go on."

"She has a place. With ocean views! And guess how much it is! Guess!"

"How much is it?"

"Twelve hundred! And she wants to give it to us."

"But in her house? Have you seen her house?"

"I know, I know," Siri laughed. "But *she showed it to me.* Come on!"

"Now?"

"It's now or never!"

Siri and I moved in right away to the top floor of the Queen's palace—our bedroom flanked by those wooden dolphins, Saint Francis greeting us at the front door.

Siri was right too. Downstairs, the Queen's house remained creatively organized. A silent character named Paul slept on the living room couch and seemed practically part of the furniture. Rotten Robbie, an ex-con and recovering alcoholic who prided himself on never drinking water and storing guns under his bed, lived in a tiny closet room next to Paul. You had to stumble over the occasional chicken to get to our stairwell. Pete then often greeted you before you went up, insisting you look one more time at his photos from a trip to China.

But Paul couldn't hurt a flea. Pete was guaranteed to make you laugh. Robbie promised to guard the house if any addicts who had failed the Queen's recovery program came back trying to rob the place. Once upstairs, you were in a new world. The room was three times the square footage of most city studios with high ceilings and skylights.

Skylights.

The central room opened into a long kitchen, which opened onto an east-facing wooden deck that hovered over the garden. The west side of the room opened into a dormer that was long enough to be a separate bedroom, a bedroom that looked out at the Pacific.

It wasn't exactly like the place we'd burned in the fire. It was far better.

Siri found beat-up antique dressers people were giving away, then sanded them and painted them teal or sage. She found a Victorian door with delicate cracks in the chipping white paint, an art piece in itself. We propped the door against the western wall—our port to let the sea inside. As we decorated, for the first time in our relationship, there was zero temptation to flee. I even felt a little settled in my job.

Not that arrows weren't still zinging everywhere, sticking out of the closet and my computer and my van's old tires. I still got anxious.

But we were in a new space for a time. Prayers answered.

19

*He who tries to shine
dims his own light.
He who defines himself
can't know who he really is.*

—LAO TZU

iri and I had quite a few dinner parties in the Queen's palace. Sometimes Carol would even show up, smelling of bonfire smoke and ozone, cackling away. Friends, most of whom could afford homes without people sleeping in the living room closets, often praised our place, and we had to pinch ourselves. Here we were, two people who couldn't write code if our lives depended on it—*and did you open the shutters? Did you smell the salt?*

Siri continued teaching. I continued writing. Work was still work. Good sometimes. Difficult often. But at the Queen's I felt that I was learning, filtering, integrating all this life info. Unlike in New York where I tried to see everything as meditation in place of *actual* meditation, this time I kept that up too. Unlike in Mexico, where I chased tubes to the exclusion of other riches, I stopped obsessing

205

rabidly about those too—perhaps that was why the tube I'd long been searching for finally sought me out.

It was a fairly awful surf day when it happened. Gloomy skies. Cold black water. Onshore winds. Rain. I was the only one paddling out near the windmill at Lawton Street and was only doing this to get some exercise.

But once out, the waves feathering far outside turned out to be protecting the inner breakers from the wind. There was a clean, organized pocket—a kind of sanctuary that you couldn't see well from anywhere until you were in the middle of it.

Inside this sanctuary, the rollers re-formed into "double-ups," waves in which two or three swells gather into one, creating more momentum and thickness.

These two- and three-headed denizens looked like beings from an Icelandic reef. But with the sky near black with rain and the winds howling, the peaks weren't inviting. They were frightening, especially because I was out alone on a tiny new board.

I thought for a minute about going in, unsure that I needed to get beaten up alone. But I figured I'd be frustrated with myself if I didn't even try. So I just bobbed around for a while, almost going on a few, then second-guessing.

Twenty minutes in, I was considering paddling in for a warm cup of tea, waveless, when a swell seemed to focus in on me. It was a strange being, a triangular peak with a squared-off, foamy head. A liquid bulldog.

Honestly, the wave didn't look like it would be much of a ride. But hoping this would be my train to the sand, I turned to paddle, made it to my feet, and the bulldog lunged. In a blink, the water beneath gutted out, and I was standing inside the most gaping, hollow cavern of salt water I'd ever witnessed from the inside. I barely needed to crouch as I whooshed through the dark belly, foam twirling around like a maypole.

As opposed to that wave at Padang, today I was going right, chest to the wall, centered—or so I felt—like Jimmy. The light at the end of the tunnel seemed far away, and I thought for certain I'd be swallowed, mashed into the blackness. But the new board—a board Jimmy had inspired me to seek out—skimmed through, never surrendering speed.

One second I was disappearing into darkness. The next, there I was under open sky, laughing. Hooting. Delirious with shock and joy in the sideways rain.

In Bali, crafty locals had gotten wise to surf vanity. They sat on the beach snapping photos. Images of nearly any wave could be purchased and posted to the globe on social media. I admit to have succumbed to this attraction. But nobody saw this wave, and that seemed right. This, like the Queen's house, was a gift, a lesson. We hunt and hunt and hunt some more. But the ocean tells its own story. We are merely rippling characters. The sea may respond to our pleas, prayers, strivings. They are part of the story—pushing and refracting back. But water will not be rushed. So relax. Be humble. Stay open. Look where others don't. There are secret sanctuaries everywhere, places nobody can tell you how to find—places you won't discover until you're there.

But the tube, as I've been trying not-so-subtly to point out, is just the metaphor. I've really been using this whole book as a way of discussing nonduality, the divinity that unites us, and how that might be integrated into this world of strip malls and melting ice caps. So it seems I should end this book on some great integrative note—like that time I actually ended suffering for good by seeing oneness forever in everyone, and never got angry again.

I'm not going to do that. I'm a father of three boys under five. The last time I got angry was this morning when our four-year-old was trying to put the baby in the toilet.

There is, however, a moment I can point to which, like that tube, gets to the heart of what I'm trying to say. So here it is, unfiltered. The beginning of the end.

Bali had reminded me that if I was going to survive modern American work life, I needed to treat myself like a car. I had to change the oil quarterly. I had to do those retreats even more often than I thought I needed them because once you *feel* your car is short on oil, the engine is already getting shredded.

A few months into living at the Queen's, that Ch'an teacher I'd been training with since my monastery days, Steven Tainer, announced that he would be teaching a weeklong dream-yoga retreat in Canada. Usually our little meditation cult did retreats near the Bay Area. But Steven had found a rare opportunity to practice at a small house on a secluded island.

After just spending all my money escaping to an island, I couldn't afford to stop working to escape to another. I told Steven I'd be missing this one. But, as you've probably gathered by now, dreams are important to me. Steven had never before given teachings on this rare form of meditation. Shortly after resigning myself to missing this retreat, I was getting coffee at my usual spot and saw a bumper sticker that said, "You miss 100 percent of the shots you don't take."

A lightbulb appeared above my head. From that café, I pitched an article on a dream-yoga retreat in Canada to *Yoga Journal*. I didn't think this would work. My travel pitches almost always got rejected. But this time, my three-pointer banked in. I was flying to Canada—a dream-yogi reporter.

Dream yoga is a practice I'd been introduced to with Sonam but had never delved into. Basically, it means dreaming lucidly, or knowing you're dreaming while you're still asleep.

Lucid dreaming has gained popularity in the West as

a psychological tool. Before flying to the retreat, I got to interview many of the country's sleep and dream scientists and psychologists. These folks told me lucid dreaming can help boost our creativity, break addictions, transcend phobias, and improve performance in sports and at work. The method, researchers said, probably works like creative visualization does—only more powerfully, because dreams feel more real.

If you interpret a nightmare about a monster to be fear about a relationship, making that mental association can be therapeutic. But in a lucid dream, you can confront or change the monster itself. "When you escape from a nightmare by waking up, you haven't dealt with the problem," Stephen LaBerge, a psychophysiologist and one of the leading dream experts, told me. "But staying with the nightmare and accepting its challenge, as lucidity makes possible, allows you to resolve the dream problem in a way that leaves you healthier than before."

In the late 1970s, LaBerge's research at Stanford University showed lucid dreaming to be both a common phenomenon and a teachable skill. "Yogis never needed any knowledge about neurology to do this," he told me. "But it's important that we do the scientific research so we can talk to Westerners about it in their own language."

After LaBerge, I interviewed a rock singer who practiced singing in his lucid dreams to expand his vocal range, a scientist who told me he'd healed his swollen tonsils in a lucid dream, and a psychologist who said she'd had sex with everyone she'd ever wanted to in lucid dreams—including herself. "It's just as much fun," she said. "And great birth control."

Dream yoga, however, is not just lucid dreaming for fun and self-improvement. Having been refined over the centuries by Tibetans and Taoists, dream yoga is used to extend mindfulness into the realm of the unconscious. Chinese and Tibetan yogis, believing that the dream body is better able to feel subtle channels and chakras, have used lucid dreaming to do physical yoga and meditation during sleep, to communicate with spiritual teachers, and for full awakening—to see that all reality is something like a dream.

Reality did seem dreamy when I made it to the Canadian island. Though only thirteen square miles, Pender Island, one of the Southern Gulf Islands, was the most beautiful thirteen miles of earth I'd ever set foot on. Forested farmlands and rocky coves reflected in the glassy Puget Sound. Pods of orcas wove through water, their massive black fins like hooks knitting silk.

This sounds like a bourgie spa week. And it was fairly plush. But Steven, following the old tradition, taught by donation. He always held his retreats in common houses where we cooked our own meals, and this was no exception. The reason we were all the way up here on a tiny dot of rock in Canada was that Steven was also a master of what you might call psychological feng shui, finding environments that were conducive to different practices. Surrounded by serene waters, swooping bald eagles, and silence, Pender was uniquely conducive to dreaming awake. After strolling around the island to marvel at the goat and llama farms above the sea, I saw his point. Pender seemed to me like the perfect spot for lots of tea and an extremely long nap.

A little too conducive. For the first couple nights I slept so deeply I couldn't remember any dreams, let alone lucid ones. But I wasn't alone. Our small group, which had become even smaller for this Canadian trip, included a physicist, a comic book writer, a retired teacher, and a hip-hop artist. All of us lived busy urban lives and felt that we needed a month of sleep retreat just to catch up. So, Steven dialed back expectations. He told us to sleep a lot and just relax without much of a schedule. He also suggested carrying a dream journal around even for naps because the more dreams you write down, the more you'll remember. Though individual dreams will often seem crazy or nonsensical, over time you notice patterns. "Your nature," Steven said, "is trying to reveal something to you."

Steven usually spoke in simple, even cryptic, terms like this. But the simplicity hid a great merging of a complex body of yogic practices—particularly the Tibetan and Chinese yogic systems Steven had spent a lifetime studying. Steven had spent his first decades of practice working with a series of revered Tibetan lamas. They'd wanted to make him a teacher, but instead, he felt he wanted to expand his knowledge and spent an equal amount of time studying Ch'an and Taoism with Chinese masters. For a few years, he even lived as a mountain hermit, practicing a Taoist yoga that is meant to be done both while awake and in dream. "It's much more efficient while you're dreaming though," Steven said casually, as if this was quite common.

Steven knew countless methods for lucidity (*The Tibetan Yogas of Dream and Sleep* is one of the best books on the subject), but we only had a couple weeks, so he taught us beginners just a few basics. Throughout the day, he recommended we inquire, "Am I dreaming?" This method worked in two ways. If you got in the habit then asked the question when you actually were dreaming, you'd become lucid right away. But asking the question while awake worked like a koan. Are we collectively dreaming *all this*?

"A bodhisattva," says the Vimalakirti Sutra, "should regard all living beings as a wise man regards the reflection of the moon in water or as magicians regard men created by magic. He should regard them as being like a face in a mirror; like the water of a mirage."

This reality-is-dream insight is something Steven and all yogic masters have said we need to experience to actually *get*. You can't just practice intellectual Zen and say "Nothing is real." That's nihilistic. But one of Steven's oldest students was that particle physicist I mentioned. George Weissman got his PhD at Berkeley, was writing a book on quantum mechanics, and loved to luxuriate in intellectual Zen. I do too sometimes. So between meditation sessions, George and I got into discussing what this "reality-is-dream theory" might mean from a physics perspective.

With his disheveled-scientist hair and Swiss-German accent, George told me that, until about a hundred years ago, scientists thought they had a decent handle on what matter is. But today we know that there is no such thing as solid matter. All this bricks-and-mortar stuff breaks down into space and tiny nonlocatable waves and particles of sub-atomic energy that we're still trying to understand. What's more, simple observation or measurement seems to change how these wavelike LEGOs of existence function.

"The theories are highly controversial," George said. "But there is no question for me that mind and matter are connected at the root."

This does not mean, George said, that reality exists in our brains, or that humans need to exist for reality to exist. Instead, material existence—or what we experience as material existence—seems to be the expression and reflection of a sort of *universal* mind that our individual minds channel and refract into the three-dimensional prism we live in. "You don't need a radio to create sound waves," George said. "The sound waves are already there. The radio is simply a structure that channels what was already there. Humans are a bit like radios."

George got into the weeds of quantum theory with me, none of which I will describe here because I don't understand it. But given that I was on a secluded island with a bunch of eccentrics talking about dreaming your way to enlightenment, it was nice to know that, scientifically speaking, we weren't totally nuts.

★ ★ ★

Steven could geek out on science too. But on retreat, he liked to keep things practical. As our primary practice, he had us doing a meditation in which we counted our breaths as we fell asleep. With each breath, we also imagined a small drop of light, like a snowflake, descending from the crown of the head to the heart center. This seemed impossible at first. I kept falling asleep before getting to five. But once I rested up, by day three or four, I could get to twenty, then fifty, then sometimes a hundred. And though it didn't produce any lucid dreams, as I lay there watching these snowflakes settle in my heart, I started to feel that eternal OKness of retreat.

But there was also something different about this sleep practice compared to usual meditation. In those rare moments when awareness trickled between sleep and waking, a space the Tibetans say mimics the transition of the mind at death, the boundaries that usually structured awareness seemed to unwind. This space was more huge and wild: a world that, like Dalí's clocks, could melt everything I thought I knew.

Then, on the fifth night, it worked. I was in old Hong Kong. Bandits were chasing me through alleys and ancient streets. I was terrified, running frantically through restaurants and strangers' homes. But just as I was tearing through someone's laundry drying between brick apartments, I saw an old African American woman knitting in the middle of the street. She was humming a beautiful tune, and there was something a little off about this picture, something that made me realize, *Oh, yeah, I'm dreaming.* I turned around, faced the bandits, then proceeded to break down walls and windows with some kung fu worthy of *Crouching Tiger, Hidden Dragon* (something I cannot pretend to do in waking life). Most of the bandits fled. The ones who didn't I beat up while the old woman cheered me on.

I woke up excited to have had some success. But in some ways, the success backfired. The next day, I wasn't present. I felt hungry for more lucid dreams. That night I dreamt I was looking for lucid dreams at a grocery store like boxes of cereal. I told Steven about this and he laughed. "We have to remember that there's nothing inherently special about lucid dreaming," he said. "Just like there's nothing inherently special about meditation. These are just tools. Don't make the tool what you're chasing."

So I tried to let go of my panicky search. It was enough to be up here on the island, I told myself. That night, I ended up at a picnic; old oak trees and patterned cloths were spread over an open meadow. People were nibbling on cheese and chocolate and fresh-baked breads. Children were playing. It was lovely. But something didn't feel quite right. The body I inhabited was unfamiliar, like a shell. After clumsily stumbling around the meadow, I realized I was actually inside some cardboard boxes strung together with string. More disconcertingly, these boxes *were* my body.

Shaken, I felt my face and became terrified. Where were my lips, my eyes, my ears? *Where was I?*

I felt out of sorts until, all of a sudden, I realized what

the problem was: I'd always been in this boxy shell. I'd just never become aware enough to notice how limiting the boxes were. I'd never noticed that I was looking through a slit cut in a box.

With that thought, consciousness, like water pouring from bottle to stream, rushed out through the eye slit, becoming the entirety of the picnic and the trees and the sky. *Oneness* doesn't capture the experience because it conjures a disappearing act, which this was emphatically not. On the contrary, I had a body but it was loose and fluid and could see in all directions. I was finally, I thought, appearing in full form: the grass, the trees, the food, the people sipping wine and eating cheese. They were all *themselves*. But they were also all me. It seemed the most obvious and most exquisite thing, a freedom unlike any other I'd ever known because it wasn't limited by the boundaries of the idea of myself I always carried like an unconscious ID card.

In the morning, I couldn't remember any dreams and felt slightly disappointed. But later that day, after morning meditation, I went jogging on a trail above the sound and saw a grassy meadow that was reminiscent of the picnic. Suddenly, the dream came back. Just like when consciousness rushed through the eye slits of the box, again it seemed as if my body enlarged. This time the feeling was less supernatural. But it was every bit as ecstatic. I looked around me, and the bent cypress trees, the black water, the brambly blackberry bushes were all extensions of my senses.

There was nobody around, which was good because I might have run up and started hugging them and crying. But out of some nearby bushes, a puppy that looked only a few weeks old stumbled onto the road. Black and puffy like a mini grizzly bear, he nuzzled into me and yipped, trying to lick my face. I stopped to play with the pup, and as he tumbled under my hands, his innocent joy seemed to be everywhere—in the dirt and the leaves and the crisp air. I sat there with him and wept. Then I jogged back and leapt into the icy sound.

20

The Canadian puppy was a nice moment. But spiritual fulfillment is as fleeting as any sort. Home from dream life, normal life went on: happy, then sad, then dull again, then sharp.

Lucid dreams came often for a while, and that was pleasant. But soon I got tired again and those vanished too.

That said, there was a moment postretreat that I often think back on and try to use as something of a compass for my work now. So here it is, the second act of the end.

My editor had assigned a story to me about why all the black people were leaving San Francisco. This was a good story, and one I was interested in. But having found such relaxation up on the island, I felt myself resisting the grit and exhaustion of reporting. I started to complain. But as I drove through traffic one Monday to do interviews, I caught myself moaning and thought, *Come on. There must be a way to change this tired approach.* Where was that universal puppy love in Monday morning traffic?

So I pulled over my van and thought about what I could do. I thought how usually I operated as if my job was to go out and affect the world, get the job done. It was *me, me, me* struggling through the workday and through the corrupt world. I was either the superhero or the victim, depending on my mood.

So, I thought, what if I just reversed both patterns—full 180? What if, instead of this noble journalist going out to *get* the story or the writer wilting under a corrupt system of top-down corporate media, what if I saw my editors and the big media conglomerate that owned our magazine and the fashion section doing puff pieces and the people I'd soon interview and my parents who'd taught me to love books and the paper mill that made our glossy pages and the printer and the trees and the semiconductor factory that allowed my computer to be and the marketing folks who sold the whiskey ads that ultimately paid my rent—what if I saw them all as writing this article? What if I let go of everything *I* thought *I* knew and let *the everything* report and write? What if I listened so well, and shut up long enough, the story told itself to me?

This could obviously get weird. *I'm here to interview you, but I'm going to let everything ask the questions, is that OK?* I didn't do that. It's important not to act nuts as a spiritual practitioner. That doesn't help anyone. But from that day forward and for the next few weeks, I tried, as much as possible, to allow the everythingness of puppy love lead. I tried to surrender. Though I won't pretend I found reporting bliss, a few interesting things happened. For one, I nearly got shot.

★ ★ ★

I was reporting the story in Bayview Hunters Point, a part of San Francisco that, back then, was not even included on tourist maps. It was a corner of the city full of gang-ridden projects, two Superfund sites, lots of liquor stores and pawn shops, a high murder rate, and not a single grocery store. It was also the only remaining mostly black neighborhood.

The standard way to report the piece would have been to go and talk to all the demographic experts about why, from 1990 to 2000, while San Francisco's overall population increased more than 7 percent, the number of people who listed their race as African American fell from 76,343 to 58,791, a decline of 23 percent, more than any major city in the country has experienced. I'd pick an expert slant and go fill in the statistics with anecdotes from local citizens.

But as I started that process, I realized that this was the story I would have written. It was a formula and had little power because formulas just go through the motions and don't really care about people and beauty. I needed to see everyone in this story as alive as that puppy on Pender: an extension of the Everything.

So I drove into Hunters Point and told myself it was time for shoe-leather reporting. But I wasn't going to get all noble and muckraking about it. Instead, I'd just have a relaxing day in the neighborhood.

This felt strange and lazy the first day. I also felt shy. Mostly I just wrote down little details about the dilapidated projects or the blighted schools. But I came back the next day and the next, just walking around Hunters Point, and became a bit more bold each day. I started striking up spontaneous conversations at BBQ joints and liquor stores, with school teachers, gangsters, politicians, business owners, and homeless folks. Again, I won't pretend I was a Jedi being guided with each step. This was still work. But I began noticing a subtle shift. I was starting to see these interviews as meeting distant family members. The drunk on the corner who'd worked the naval shipyard and now had cancer, the fourteen-year-old hiding a sawed-off shotgun in his black 49ers puff coat, the high school basketball star who became a preacher, the cop who'd grown up in the hood before going to war in Iraq, the teacher, the rapper, the developer, the politician. They were each someone's son or daughter. Each of their stories had its own wisdom of experience—a tale worthy of Shakespeare or Byron or Joyce if you stayed long enough. I soon met Kev.

According to a survey by the San Francisco Educational Services, young people in Bayview Hunters Point tended to "maintain unrealistic expectations of stardom in sports or entertainment as the only alternative to low-end jobs." But Kev Kelley told me he was one of the lucky ones. He was going to do the impossible.

And why not? Kev had good looks and talent. Shock-G from Digital Underground was producing some of Kev's songs, and Kevin Epps, a documentary filmmaker from Bayview, was making Kev one of three stars in a documentary called *Rap Dreams*. Kev said he was friends with all the biggies. "Mistah F.A.B., Dead Prez, Shock-G. I fuck with all them," Kev told me when we met in Oakland after his grandfather, who ran a local trucking company, told me I had to meet his rap star grandson.

Kev grew up in Hunters Point, but I was meeting him at his Oakland apartment because he had recently been priced out of San Francisco when he couldn't find placement in the projects. He still represented San Francisco in all his music though. He also said he was the only one who could show me the real Hunters Point.

"This is the shit they don't talk about in the papers." He smiled. "Ride in with me."

As we drove back into the city, Kev—in a brown San Francisco Giants hat that hovered over his cornrows and the tops of his ears—went back and forth between telling gangster tales and spontaneously breaking into his raps. "Step into my soul / See what I've seen / I felt pain / I was born to get the money and the fame," he shouted out the window.

I liked Kev. He was proud, boastful. But his pride seemed rooted in wanting to give back to the community. "I'm gonna save this neighborhood with music," Kev said. "Because, see, even in Africa, black culture was always about shining. I think, being in a culture that has been so deprived, our ancestors, the youth, the coming generations, they thrive off being able to say, 'Look, this is me. Like, I came straight from Newcomb, and this is me.'"

While driving down Newcomb, an infamously violent street, Kev moaned about the gun violence that had taken so many of his friends. But when we arrived at our first destination, Rudy's Bar-b-que Pit on Third Street, as soon as we hit the sidewalk, Kev looked like a lost child who'd found home again. He began whirling around, shaking hands, giving hugs, introducing me to everyone in sight. "Tell this reporter how I'm doing this rap thing," he said to some young guys standing on the corner. They nodded and smiled. "Yeah, you doin' that."

While we chatted with this crew, a black Suburban with shiny silver rims soon pulled up on the corner in front of the BBQ shop. The driver was a middle-aged man named Muhammad, the son of the owner of a nearby gym. Kev wanted me to interview him. I still had no idea what my story was about. So I leaned into the Suburban asking Muhammad questions. Kev meanwhile went to grab some BBQ and, deep in questions, I didn't see the two silver Crown Victorias pull up behind. I did, however, hear a voice through a megaphone: "Green sweatshirt, get your hands out of your pockets!"

The megaphone startled me, but I'd been hearing sirens and cops throughout the week. I ignored them until the sounds got closer: "Get your hands out of your pockets! In the green, get your hands out of your pockets now!"

At that moment, Muhammad's eyes widened. His hands drifted to the top of his head.

"Green sweatshirt! Remove yourself from the vehicle," came the voice, which was now directly behind me, "or we will remove you from the vehicle!"

I looked at my sweatshirt. It was indeed green. But

somehow—white privilege? urban naïveté?—the words didn't register as personal until Muhammad nodded at me like, "Dude, turn the hell around!"

I turned. A short muscular African American man was standing just a couple feet from me. The veins in his arms bulged, and as I followed those bulging arms, I saw that a large silver pistol was trained on my face.

"Hands out of your pockets now!" he shouted.

I don't remember thinking at all as I looked down the barrel of that pistol. I simply found my hands rising from my pockets. I continued, however, gripping my voice recorder, *a bright, shiny metal object* that is about the size of one of those little guns you see in old British spy movies.

"Drop the weapon now!" the man said.

Weapon? The word ping-ponged about my brain without meaning.

Fortunately, Kev had just popped out of the BBQ joint with his ribs and had seen this too many times. "The fucking recorder, Jaimal! Drop that shit! Drop that motherfucking recorder!"

Kev's voice broke my brain freeze. I dropped the recorder and realized seven plainclothes cops had surrounded us. Before I knew it, I was being pressed against the cop car and searched.

I tried to act calm while the cops patted us down. Everyone else was acting calm. Everyone but Kev. "He's a reporter," Kev kept shouting with the same exuberance he rapped with. The cop who had pulled the gun, Officer Scott, didn't look as though he was buying it. This pissed

Kev off. "This is why I brought him here," Kev said, "just so he can experience firsthand what we go through every day. Cause it shows what it means to be in the neighborhood, that's all. With this face!"

Scott, who was black too, shot Kev a "don't pull that with me" look. "I don't discriminate," he said, and told Kev he was going to give him a ticket for loitering. We debated whether Kev and I were loitering or not, and Officer Scott told us that he had a room full of guns confiscated from this exact corner. "This is not just any corner to be standing on Kev," he said. "You know this."

Kev rolled his eyes, but eventually, after calling in to see if Kev had any warrants—he didn't—the cops let us go.

The Crown Victorias sped off. Safely inside Rudy's Barb-que Pit, Kev hollered to the whole place that I just had my first gun pulled on me. He thought this was hysterical.

"I told you," Kev shouted, "the police out here are totally racist. They are hating on anyone from the community with any success. They will ride by you twenty times in two hours. It just makes no sense. I mean, go investigate a murder. Do something with your time instead of harassing."

As we ate, I tried to laugh with Kev, to act part of the scene. I didn't feel rattled. I didn't even blame Officer Scott or the gangsters who might have had those guns for Scott to confiscate any other day. You could smell the blood in the air in Hunters Point and the cops and the robbers were both channeling the stress. I was just glad Scott didn't shoot.

Kev and I went on to have a normal day in the neighborhood before going to have shrimp and grits with his grandfather, who only laughed when I told him the story. "Welcome to the neighborhood, son," he said.

By this point I did feel part of the neighborhood. I felt that I could be any of the cops or teachers or shipyard workers or Kev. But later that night, as Siri and I cooked spring pasta in our little beach loft, our ever-gentrifying white coast, I found myself getting choked up. Maybe it was Siri's reaction to the story—"You could've been killed!" Maybe it was sadness for the kids who had to grow up with guns as ordinary as baseballs in the self-proclaimed "most liberal" city on earth. But as I conjured the image of Officer Scott holding that pistol to my face, the experience was a bit like becoming lucid in a dream.

It was an ordinary Tuesday night dinner, and the world turned vivid like the picnic dream. Our wooden thrift-store dining room table, Siri's abstract paintings, even the sound of our voices over the traffic. They all hit me at once. It was clear that this was what was important.

What was important exactly? I wasn't sure I could say, but I suppose it was all these little things that were our fingers and toes and hair and eyes and how beautiful they could be. The way the zucchini and squash sat with the fusilli, looking inviting on the blue plate with chipped edges. The way Siri's bangs lay against her forehead and her green-gray eyes had been placed right there in her skull. The way the wooden floorboards creaked when you stepped on them.

We all know that we could go any day: a car accident, a brain aneurysm, a heart attack, a bullet. Rich and poor, black and white, gay and straight, nothing protects us. We know this, and yet we don't *know it*. We move through life as if we have forever, as if we can take the stroll around the block, the cappuccino made unusually well, the Tuesday fusilli, for granted. We live as if there will always be a million more like this. So we filter out the details. We go on stressing about accumulating achievements, the big impressive things. But the big impressive things we hold up as the meaning of it all—success, the house on the hill, the shiny car, the World Series title—the things we decide are worth filtering out the little things for—are they so great? Is winning so unique and pleasant? Is success so supreme? Are shiny cars that lovely? They're OK, sure.

But that night I saw Officer Scott had given me a gift. He'd made me recall briefly that nothing beats spring pasta on Tuesday with your girlfriend, the sensation of breath in your lungs, a walk on the dunes after dinner, the full moon sinking behind the city.

21

Ananda: *"This is half of the holy life, lord: admirable friendship, admirable companionship, admirable camaraderie."*
Buddha: *"Don't say that, Ananda. Don't say that. Admirable friendship, admirable companionship, admirable camaraderie is actually the whole of the holy life."*

—UPADDHA SUTTA

What was also nice about almost getting shot by Officer Scott was that I decided it wasn't worth stressing too much about writing the article either. I tried as much as possible to let the people I'd interviewed tell the story, to hear their voices coming through, to let the story tell itself.

The story ended up being the longest and most quickly written magazine piece I've ever written. It's also the only article I've ever written that won an award of any note. And when it did, I was happy. But I didn't really feel surprised or even proud. The success didn't feel like mine. I had been one piece of the story. The scribe. A small piece really. A pawn.

★ ★ ★

For a while I felt able to work from this more easygoing place. But everything changes. When the sea has been calm and glassy, you can bet a storm is rolling in. I was starting to realize this, I suppose, and subsequent minor life hurricanes would go, more or less, like this. First book would come out, and I'd nearly have a panic attack that it was the wrong book. Siri would leave me, and I'd feel like God was running a lawn mower over my aortas. Second book would come out, and I'd have another panic attack. Pa would get cancer, and we'd spend our days wondering why we waited so long to appreciate our father.

There are cycles. Some patterns repeat. Some are shocking flash floods. But here is the thing about storms. I don't wish them on you, but they are coming and would you want it differently? What would we talk about? How would we become strong? How would we get off our lazy asses and look into what is actually going on here? What would we celebrate? Storms, after all, have that rare power to bring us—yes, we humans who love to devour each other and put it on TV to watch again—together. Neighbors who have never met are suddenly sharing a lifeboat, giving each other coffee and potatoes.

I have been spoiled in this life by mostly sunny weather. But I'd like the third act of this ending to briefly mention the minor storm—really more of a squall—that reunited me with an old friend.

About a year after writing that journalism story about black San Francisco, I'd finally finished my book *Saltwater*

Buddha. I'd tried as much as possible to learn and let the story write me, but as I was finishing my book, I was also reading Tim Winton, an Australian novelist with a brooding and dark aesthetic, an aesthetic uniquely his and beautiful. Usually, I could separate my love of other writers from my own style. The problem was that Winton wrote about the sea. Worse, he surfed. I was beginning to hate him.

"The poison of the honeybee is the artist's jealousy," wrote Blake. I knew this. But this honeybee had hit in the fattiest part of my ass. In other words, I didn't feel a sting. But jealousy permeated subtly. Deep.

The more I compared my rather sunny book to Winton's dark, brooding sea, the more I knew I'd done this all wrong. This led me down a rabbit hole of opening dozens of great novels and memoirs and comparing myself to them, which is the death of creativity. You can gain inspiration from other artists, but if you look to them trying to have their voice or popularity, you will only regurgitate them poorly. I thought I knew that. But with this bee-sting venom coursing through my veins, I got amnesia. All I could see was that this Winton perspective, combined with shrewd vocabulary and sentence structure, could lead to literary fame. I muzzled all those insights from the dream-yoga retreat and reporting with Kev—or twisted them—and I chased down Winton.

★ ★ ★

So, even though Siri was saying that she liked my book as it was, and my publisher had said the same, I proceeded to go in and change everything.

There was some OK writing in the new draft. But I'd later realize—after much suffering—that the new version lacked power because some fabricated new ego had written a formula.

I sent the new draft off to the publisher thinking, *Ha! Wait until they see this. This will really knock their socks off if they liked it before.*

It did not knock their socks off.

"We don't want this book," my editor told me, his jaw sounding tight. "You know, we liked the old book—the book that seemed, well, seemed like *you*."

There is little more frustrating than doing months of work and then having your boss tell you that all the work you just did would have been better off not done. You do not get those months back.

So, even though part of me agreed with this editor, I silenced this part of me and became angry and righteous. I told the publisher, "Well, I don't want to publish that old book. I can't. I'm going to return the money."

"That would be a shame," they said. "But OK."

"Well, it's what I'm going to do," I said, feeling noble.

I went on like this for another couple of months, brooding and thinking I'd been wronged, censored. I was in a manic mood as I started searching for another publisher who would appreciate my work. Some possibilities opened, then closed, then opened, then closed.

So I went back to magazine writing, working overtime to try to make up the money I would have to pay the publisher. Siri and I even did some day-trading, but this was 2008, so you can guess how that went.

Over the couple of months that this ridiculous lifestyle lasted—waking at 6:00 a.m. with Wall Street—my moods were up and down like the stock market. No inner stability. I talked to Siri often about quitting writing altogether and learning to do something practical: bagging groceries, building websites. I didn't care. I was turning on writing because it was turning on me.

Fortunately Rotten Robbie still lived downstairs.

Rotten Robbie painted houses for money, but the work was sporadic. The fact that he looked as if he just got out of prison didn't help. Often, when he didn't have work, he just sat out in front of Carol's chain-smoking and drinking Rockstar energy drinks and coffee. I'm not kidding that he didn't drink water. Not a drop. He looked sixty years old— hair and mustache bright white—even though he was only thirty-seven.

Rob had a hard exterior. He constantly bragged about his plethora of guns, his childhood in the ghetto, his jail time. But Siri and I had both developed a soft spot for Rob. When you got to know him, you saw that all Rob really wanted, like most of us, was some friends—some people to protect and love, a family like the one he'd had in his gangster days.

Only now he wasn't a gangster and was having a little trouble adjusting to the vocabulary and lifestyle of law-abiding citizens. He was, thanks to the Queen, trying hard though. Staying away from the bottle and the drugs. Working any job. Even his occasional racist slur was prison theatrics. It turned out that his best friends were black and Mexican. "Yeah, man," Rob would say, "the *vatos* I used to ride with. Those were the fucking days, brother! We had a fucking Impala you wouldn't believe. Bitches. Money. Everything. But once you're in the joint, you got nobody but your own."

You get the picture. Sometimes when Rob was out smoking, I'd sit with him. I didn't smoke, but for bonding purposes, I'd bum a cigarette and listen to stories from his criminal days.

Usually, Rob just rambled for twenty minutes and then I left him to his tobacco and coffee. But one sunny day, after I'd been pummeled good by big surf, I walked up dripping wet, head hanging, and Rob said, "Well, what are you looking so sullen about, you dick?"

I wasn't looking sullen because of how badly I'd just been beaten up by Ocean Beach. I was feeling sullen, I told Rob, because I was going to quit writing. I'd recently gotten an offer from a friend to work in advertising and thought I'd give it a go.

"We live in San Francisco," I said. "What am I trying to prove by being poor, you know?"

Rob knew how much I loved writing because he'd gotten to know me when I was looking at it positively, but I was still expecting him to say, "Yeah, yeah, go get that money. Get the money and bitches. That's what life's about."

That was sort of his mantra. But instead he gave me an angry look, a look as if I'd offended his soul.

"Are you fucking with me?" he said.

"No, man," I said. "I just don't see the point of the struggle. The high school down the street is tearing down its library because the kids just do their work online. What am I doing trying to write books?"

Rob put his cigarette out on the sidewalk slowly, then he turned to me, looked me dead in the eyes, and pushed me hard in the chest. I nearly fell into Carol's planter boxes. We wrestled briefly as we often did, but Rob was more serious than usual. He pushed me hard again.

"Hey, motherfucker," he said. "Stop. Look at me."

Rob lifted up his sleeves, revealing his gang tattoos, scars from knife fights and gunshots.

"You think this shit is easy," he said. "You think *life*— this fucking hellhole—is supposed to be *easy*. This shit ain't easy. But you don't fucking quit like a little bitch. You think it's easy for me not to get plastered right now? I fucking fight it every second. And I don't know much. I didn't get a fancy education. But I know this. Don't be a fucking sellout. Look at you, up there on the top floor. A girlfriend.

Writing stories on your fucking laptop all creative and shit. Going fucking surfing. You know what would happen to me if I swam out there? I'd drown. I don't know how to fucking swim. I'd love to be out there, but I never got that chance. I never had a dad teach me shit. I'd love to write stories, but I never got an education. I'm down here living in the fucking closet, spouting off about stupid shit I used to do like I'm a Vietnam war hero. But you've got a chance. It's not too late for you, you stupid punk-ass bitch. So don't fucking be a sellout, you fucktard."

I took a drag, tried not to cough, and looked away. Rob was making good sense to me. I even was a little choked up. But I didn't want to let Rob know he was getting to me. Also I'd made up my mind. It was time to get real. Get practical.

"Yeah," I said. "Maybe."

"Hey," Rob said. "Don't start. Do not fucking start this 'maybe' bullshit, one foot in, one foot out. That shit gets you nowhere. Hey, for me. I'm asking you *for me*. Look at these eyes. *Do not be a little bitch*."

Now, Rob's speech might sound especially dramatic and offensive. But this was actually how Rob talked all the time. To everyone. Most people ran the other way or called the cops. But Rob, if you could get past the harsh facade, had a kind of wisdom. He really had been to hell and back. He'd seen where poor choices led. This time seemed a little different from his usual ranting.

I looked at Rob in the eyes—his bloodshot, tired, bright blue eyes. They were welling up slightly. Rob seemed to genuinely mean what he was saying. He seemed to care. I took another drag.

"OK," I said. "Maybe you're right."

"Ha-ha!" Rob shouted. "Victory! I should be a fucking motivational speaker or some shit. Now put me in one of your stories, dickwad—make me famous!"

I didn't decide to go back to my book. I was convinced that it was a bad idea. But I decided to keep going with journalism and passed on advertising. (Not that there's anything wrong with that career, by the way. It's just not for me.)

Anyway, it was about a month later that I received the call I spoke of at the start of this book, a call from a New York number.

I almost never pick up calls from numbers I don't recognize. But on this particular day, ferocious northwest winds caking our windows with sand, I was steeped in a stack of Freedom of Information Act requests relating to private funding of public universities. Maybe I just needed an excuse to get out of the contracts. But I picked up the phone and heard familiar laughter.

"Hello?" I said, briefly wondering if this was a prank call.

"Ja-ma," the voice said.

"Uh, yeah. Hello?"

"Ja-ma!"

"Who is this?"

"Dis Sonam. *I here. I here. America!*"

"Sonam!" I shouted, leaping out of my seat. I hadn't heard his voice in more than four years.

"What! How! When! Are you here? Are you in California?"

Sonam laughed for a while, then said, "No, no. I here New York. Dis many many work."

"That's great," I said, still in disbelief. "I mean, I think it's good. Are you OK? I was worried. I didn't hear from you."

"Ya, ya, sorry," Sonam said. "Dis go South India tree year. Many time no computer. I sorry no write, Ja-ma."

"But you're OK?" I said.

"Ya, ya, good. Bery happy," Sonam said.

He paused.

"But, Ja-ma. You right. Dis America life bery busy."

He cracked up again. I laughed too.

"Told you so," I said.

"But I so happy now talk you. You still best friend, Ja-ma. I tink we still one day Tibet going."

Misty-eyed, I began pacing around the flat. I didn't know where to begin, so I started firing off questions before Sonam could fully answer them. We talked for an hour—even sang one "Country Roads" chorus.

Apparently, Sonam had come to New York with a delegation of Tibetan monks accompanying a lama. But when they returned to India, Sonam stayed on, finding the job he'd always hoped for in a Tibetan restaurant, one that paid next to nothing but, with a monk's frugality, was still allowing him to send money home to his family.

"Wait, wait—what!" I said. "You mean you found them, Sonam? You found your family!"

"Ya, ya," he said casually. "I try go see family now."

Sonam's village had gotten a phone. Through a distant cousin in the US, he'd found the number. When he called the first two times, he said, he could only talk to his sister because his mother cried tears of joy for a week when she found out her son was alive. But eventually, he spoke to his mother, "and she many many saying Sonam Sonam. I need see you. We cry a lot. We laugh."

Sonam's father had died, but Sonam seemed at peace with this.

"He live long," he said. "He happy."

Sonam was not, however, at peace with the news of his older brother, the first of the family to graduate high school. To support his family, the brother had become a police officer with local Chinese officials, Sonam said. But when the brother tried to defend a Tibetan who he thought had been unfairly treated, he was killed, Sonam said, by the police.

"Dis many many angry," Sonam said. "Every night tinking how help family. Tibet."

We spoke about human rights groups Sonam could get in touch with, a process he said he was already beginning, then about raising money to get Sonam home. For real this time.

It was so good to speak to him, and I wanted to stay on

the phone forever. But Sonam was spending money from his pay-by-minute cell phone. So we said good-bye, agreeing to work together to get him out to the West Coast and back to Tibet.

"I still never see ocean," Sonam said. "I tink come see Ja-ma bery soon."

"You can stay with us," I said, thinking a Tibetan monk would fit right in at the Queen's palace. (I could only imagine the conversations he and Rob would have.) "As long as you need. You live here, OK?"

"OK, OK," Sonam said. "I so happy. Bye-bye now."

I hung up the phone. The joy I had felt when Sonam and I walked those Himalayan trails together, the joy I had felt after those weeks in silence, came flooding back. I also, like the lifting of a veil, understood exactly the jealous bee sting I'd received while writing.

I'd been jealous of Winton the way I'd been jealous in the Himalayas of Jyanth. I was pining after success as I'd pined after an imagined Sati, a Sati whom I'd put on a pedestal to try to fill the emptiness in myself. But just like then, the ordinary stuff that was already here, the ordinary quirks, the ordinary cage, the ordinary me, was good on its own if I didn't resist. How many times did I have to learn this? (The answer, by the way, would be many. I am still learning every day.)

I literally ran to my drawer and dusted off my manuscript, the pre-jealous version, and read it cover to cover. I read it this time as if I were a stranger picking up this story. And I realized something. It was not Homer's *Odyssey*. But I'd done my best, and this was an honest book. It was a book in which, on my deathbed, I could say, "I said what was true in my experience." That, I realized, was worth more than saying anything half true for lots of money.

I wrote my publisher the next morning.

"If it's not too late to change my mind, I'd like to say, you're right. I'm an idiot. The old book is better."

The editor called minutes later.

"What's going on with you?" he asked. "You seemed so sure."

"I don't know," I said. "But I got a call from an old friend. He helped me see straight."

"Well, I'm glad," the editor said. "Congratulations."

Just like that, a flick of the mind, I did not owe back my book advance. I could stop day-trading. And maybe help Sonam get home.

That call from Sonam was almost eight years ago. As I mentioned in the introduction, I hoped to take these stories up to present day. But somewhere along the line, I realized that this book was Sonam's book—an homage to my old best friend and teacher.

Still, it's nice to end current. Today is Saturday. My lovely wife, Amy—who I met just a year after Siri and I broke up, a year that is covered in another book—is nursing Hanafin, our third boy, who has made it out of her belly safely after, as you may recall, a few scares. I'm taking Kaifas and Eben across the street to the beach, and as usual, the little gurus (ages four and two) offer a teaching.

The waves are thunderous today, apartment-building high and stormy. Too big for anyone to surf. Dangerous undertow. So the boys and I play in the glops of foam and search for sand crabs.

Eben, the younger, has not learned fear yet. Repeatedly he runs into the violent waters.

"Stop already!" I shout after his fourth attempt. "It's too big today."

"No!" Eben screams, running toward the churn.

I chase him, scoop him up.

"You have to wait till you're bigger," I say.

"I'm already bigger," Eben shouts.

Then I have to tickle torture him. Laughter is often the only way.

We return to our sand crab moat. Kaifas, looking self-satisfied that he did not get scolded, says, "I like small waves, Dadu."

"You do?" I say. "What do you like better though? Big waves or small waves?"

"I like all waves," he says.

It's a good gig, parenting. A time you realize everyone must be forgiven forever and ever because we all went through dealing with *our parents*. When your toddlers are climbing on you at 5:30 a.m. and you haven't slept in three days and the coffee doesn't work anymore and your sentences aren't quite forming and your wife reminds you that you didn't get half-and-half or toilet paper yesterday like you said you would, well, you know all should be forgiven. Always and forever. In the words of Rotten Robbie, "This shit ain't easy."

But at least we are in the same sinking boat, humans. Nobody gets a lifeboat until we all do.

After some friends and I raised a bit of money for Sonam but once again failed to get him home, Sonam called me a few years ago, saying he'd left his vows, had gone and gotten married, had a baby, and was now, while living in Queens, broke and unable to send money home anymore.

"I still good, Ja-ma," he said. "But I tink dis parent life America bery hard."

I agreed. I wanted to make things better. I tried to get a book proposal together about Sonam and I returning to Tibet to see his family. And many times I thought it was the right time. But in the middle of each attempt, something would thwart me.

I spoke to Sonam the last time a couple years ago and was finally planning a visit to New York to meet his family. But then Eben was born. Then we were moving. I delayed and delayed. Sonam doesn't even really live in the modern world. Email is something he catches up on once per year. I'm not much better. By the time I could finally go to New York, Sonam had stopped responding to both calls and emails. He was not on social media, and still is not.

I have not been able to find him through our few old mutual friends in India, and about 20 percent of the Tibetan population is named Sonam.

Did Sonam finally go home to Tibet? Is he working too hard? Did he go too far in trying to find justice for his brother? I don't know. But I know we will find each other when the time is right. I also don't worry about Sonam. He is wise. He will land on his feet.

Still, I miss him. I want Amy and our boys to know him and meet his family. I want them to know the peace of those songs and hikes in McLeod.

So, if you meet a very happy Tibetan father named Sonam Wangdue—he apparently grew his hair long like one of those Tibetan warriors—please tell him to call Ja-ma. My phone number has not changed. I even sometimes check the old Yahoo email. Tell him that you read his story. That I'm grateful to have learned from him. And that I many many pray we Tibet going soon.

A Brief Note on "Reality"

Books are lies. This one is no different. Our memories fool us. Recent neuroscience suggests that the more we remember an event the more we change that event in our minds. Memoirists are doomed. To boot, language—being a symbolic representation of a thing or idea, a thing or idea that must be re-conjured by the reader's faulty memories and faulty senses—can never represent reality. Nevertheless, language is what we have. It can be beautiful. And it's possible, I think, to use language to point toward truth. That is what I've tried to do here. The stories are real and true to my memories of actual events. The facts have been checked. That said, I'm sure there are plenty of places where my memories, or language representing those memories, miss the mark. Also, there are places where I knowingly warped time. The section on Robert Thurman is the most imaginary. I attended a number of Thurman's lectures at Columbia, as well as listened to a number of his recorded talks, and took in all the information I describe. Thurman's words had the effects on me I describe and catalyzed the reflection on death I describe. But Thurman never went on that specific long-winded tangent in his class when I was there. For the narrative, I bottled the thrust of the message, and the feeling I experienced, into one lecture. And to stay accurate, I quoted his introduction to his own translation of *The Tibetan Book of the Dead: The Great Book of Natural Liberation* (the best translation I've yet to read). I'm grateful to Dr. Thurman and Bantam Books for allowing me to use the passage.

The second place I warp time is in Bali. I've made four trips to Made's over the last decade, adding up to about a year there. Jimmy has been there each time and we have surfed hundreds of waves together. Perhaps it's the ethereal nature of that place, but those waves and conversations have blurred together to the point that I can't remember what was said when, which waves were ridden when. All of the things I describe in that chapter happened, but I collapsed time once again, partly because I can't recall the exact order, partly to help the story arch.

ACKNOWLEDGMENTS

S ome of the stories in this book include adaptations from articles published in *San Francisco Magazine*, *Yoga Journal*, the *Surfer's Journal*, and *Shambhala Sun* (now the *Lion's Roar*). I'm grateful to all of the editors at those publications for the opportunity to write and for allowing me to adapt the articles for this book.

Countless people supported me through living and writing the stories contained in *All Our Waves*—too many to mention—but none more than my family, especially: my mom, Janice, who doubles as my coach, therapist, and editor; my dad, Peter, whose grace, humor, love, and honesty in facing his own death was key fuel for these words; my sister, Ciel, whose grit and compassion in getting through medical school and beyond has been a constant inspiration; and my stepmom, Margaret, who doubles as my social media publicist and never fails to get me laughing when I need it. I owe the biggest debt of gratitude to my wife, Amy, who encourages these quixotic endeavors (and helps edit them) while literally helping cure cancer by day, keeping our calendar in order, and being a ridiculously stellar mom. Can we get a date night soon, honey?

To our boys—Kaifas, Eben, Hanafin—if you ever decide to pick this dusty book off the shelf and see what your gray-haired dad was up to when you were just twinkles, know that, even though I loved my time rambling solo around the globe and am profoundly grateful for the opportunity to write books, I'll never have a job that's more enlightening or that I'm more proud of than being your dad. Every day you remind me what's most important—and that if you keep your compass on love you'll always end up on the best island. May you learn from your dad's mistakes.

Of course, I also want to thank all the characters in this book. My memories and writing, I know, fall far short of being able to reflect who you really are or the experiences we shared. Thank you for putting up with my best shot. Thank you also to Karen Rinaldi, Hannah Robinson, Harper Wave, and HarperCollins for having faith in this project from its foggy beginnings, and for your combination of openheartedness and shrewd intellectual discernment. I'll paddle out with you anytime.

ABOUT THE AUTHOR

Jaimal Yogis is an award-winning writer, outdoorsman, and frequent teacher. He is the author of the memoir *Saltwater Buddha*, which has been made into a feature documentary film, and *The Fear Project: What Our Most Primal Emotion Taught Me About Survival, Success, Surfing and Love*. A graduate of Columbia Journalism School, he has written for *ESPN: The Magazine*, the *Washington Post*, the *Chicago Tribune*, *San Francisco Magazine*, the *Surfer's Journal*, and many other publications. He lives in San Francisco with his wife, Amy, and their three sons.